The Culture Wars of the
Late Renaissance

*The Bernard Berenson Lectures
on the Italian Renaissance*

SPONSORED BY VILLA I TATTI

HARVARD UNIVERSITY CENTER FOR

ITALIAN RENAISSANCE STUDIES

FLORENCE, ITALY

The Culture Wars of the Late Renaissance

SKEPTICS, LIBERTINES, AND OPERA

EDWARD MUIR

HARVARD UNIVERSITY PRESS

CAMBRIDGE, MASSACHUSETTS

LONDON, ENGLAND

2007

Library of Congress Cataloging-in-Publication Data

Muir, Edward, 1946–
The culture wars of the late Renaissance:
skeptics, libertines, and opera / Edward Muir.
p. cm.—
(The Bernard Berenson lectures on the Italian Renaissance)
"Sponsored by Villa I Tatti, Harvard University Center
for Italian Renaissance Studies, Florence, Italy."
Includes bibliographical references and index.
ISBN-13: 978-0-674-02481-6 (alk. paper)
ISBN-10: 0-674-02481-8 (alk. paper)
1. Venice (Italy)—History—1508–1797.
2. Venice (Italy)—Intellectual life—16th century.
3. Padua (Italy)—History—16th century.
4. Padua (Italy)—Intellectual life—16th century.
5. Renaissance—Italy—Venice.
6. Renaissance—Italy—Padua.   I. Title.
DG675.6.M76 2007
945'.3107—dc22   2006050843

Designed by Gwen Nefsky Frankfeldt

To those who have taught me the most

Donald Weinstein
and
Gene Brucker
and in memory of
William Bouwsma
and
Felix Gilbert

Contents

Illustrations

Preface

Long ago I learned to pay attention when Theodore Rabb twists my arm. In his capacity as one of the editors of the *Journal of Interdisciplinary History,* he asked me to prepare a paper on early opera in Venice for a conference he had been trying to organize for decades that would bring together historians and musicologists to discuss the history of opera. At first I balked because although I might claim to know a little something about Venice, my knowledge of opera does not stretch much beyond what one learns as a fairly ardent opera fan. I could count on one hand the number of seventeenth-century operas I had ever seen produced. My historical knowledge of Venice rapidly fades after 1607, and the first Venetian opera was not performed until 1637. Ted did not listen to my objections, and I yielded by writing a paper, "Why

Venice? Venetian Society and the Success of Early Opera," presented at a conference at Princeton in 2004 and now published in the *Journal of Interdisciplinary History* 36 (2006): 331–353.

That same spring I presented a rather different version of that paper at a Renaissance Society of America conference session dedicated to the memory of the late Patricia Labalme, a superb scholar of humanism and women's intellectual history. Patsy was a historian and lover of Venice as well as a dedicated opera fan, and the paper seemed an appropriate tribute to her. After the conference Joseph Connors, the director of the Harvard Center for Italian Renaissance Studies, asked me if I would be willing to expand the paper, to be given as the first annual Bernard Berenson Lectures at I Tatti. Such was the genesis of this little book.

Joe's invitation allowed me to explore a broader range of the cultural politics of the early seventeenth century than had been possible in the Princeton paper, especially the philosophical and literary currents in Padua and Venice from which successful commercial opera emerged. My interests soon pushed rather far beyond the origins of Venetian opera and opened onto the ideological and religious conflicts that I have chosen to call the culture wars of the late Renaissance. I wrote the lectures while I enjoyed the view over the San Francisco Bay from my study at the Center for Advanced Studies in the Behavioral Sciences in Stanford, California. I wish to thank the other fellows for listening to my lunchtime stories about the arcane world of seventeenth-century Venice, a place so alien to their very contemporary concern with understanding and improving our own world. I suppose I seemed a strange duck out of water among those hardheaded but often softhearted social scientists.

While presenting the lectures at I Tatti, I enjoyed the gracious hospitality of Françoise and Joseph Connors, the support of the magnificent I Tatti staff, and the stimulation of interaction with the lively fellows. My research assistant at Northwestern, Jonah Grabelsky, was a superb help, especially with the illustrations. In preparing the lectures and revising them for this book, I greatly benefited from advice from the members of the Chicago Renaissance seminar, hosted by David M. Bevington and Richard Strier, and the members of the Newberry Library Center for Research in Festive Culture seminar hosted by Samuel Kinser. I also wish to thank Kenneth Alder, Albert Ascoli, Anna Maria Busse Berger, Robert Bireley, S.J., Eve Borsook, Kelley Casson, Janie Cole, Beth Condie-Pugh, Joseph Connors, Alan Curtis, John A. Davis, Paula Findlen, Jane F. Fulcher, Andrea Gáldy, Julian Gardner, Christa Gardner von Teuffel, Wendy Heller, James H. Johnson, Robert Kendrick, Patrick Macey, David Peterson, David Posner, Antonella Romano, Dennis Romano, Ellen Rosand, Sarah Ross, Ethan Shagan, and as always my dearest friend and best critic, Regina Schwartz.

The Culture Wars of the
Late Renaissance

Introduction

Let him who cannot amaze
work in the stables.

Giambattista Marino

The Culture Wars of the Late Renaissance represents an attempt
to understand a moment in late-Renaissance history by re-
uniting what the modern disciplines of the history of science, philosophy, literature, religion, and music, with their
varying concerns, have tended to keep separate. An eclectic
range of cultural activities, from stargazing and philosophical commentaries to the writing of polemical satires and opera libretti, preoccupied late-Renaissance intellectuals. I have
brought together these diverse interests by paying attention
to a particular place, Venice and its satellite university city of
Padua, during a specific period. The book begins with the
Paduan student riots against the Jesuit college in 1591 and

ends with the demise of the Venetian Accademia degli Incogniti (Academy of the Unknowns) in about 1660.

During this period Venice became the center within the Catholic world of opposition to the extension of papal authority, and the home of a vibrant press that published books without significant interference from church or governmental censors. The culture wars raging around Venice pitted the defenders of Catholic orthodoxy, especially the Jesuit fathers and the Universal Roman Inquisition, against the skeptical philosophers at the University of Padua, the libertines of the Venetian academies, and the librettists of early opera. Given its power to evoke dramatic emotions, opera became the primary means for expressing and commenting on the cultural politics of the day—not just ecclesiastical politics but sexual politics, which had heated up because so few Venetian patrician men married and so many Venetian patrician women were forced into convents. The disjuncture between marriage and sexuality among the Venetian upper classes created a demographic crisis that added fuel to the culture wars. Traditional Christian culture provided little guidance for those who lived through and suffered from the collapse of marriage structures but did not have a religious vocation.

Despite their often mutual animosity, the men and women on the Venetian side of the culture wars constituted a true intellectual community, a small republic of letters, in which one generation had a formative influence on another and most of the members of each generation knew one another personally. Intimate ties of family, class, and personal knowledge bound most of the principal members of the community. They denounced their opponents with a level of vitriol that matches that of the cultural wars of our own times. Literati were harsh with one another but harsher still with their perceived enemies—the Society of Jesus, the Spanish imperialists, the Roman Inquisition, and in the later years the Barberini papacy. What makes the culture wars of the late Renaissance significant is the wide range of ideas the skeptics, libertines, and librettists explored under the protection of Venice's relatively tolerant government, which allowed the airing of almost anything, as long as its own form of aristocratic republicanism was never questioned. In several respects this moment in the late Renaissance can be seen as a kind of proto-Enlightenment, a foreshadowing of the cultural concerns of the eighteenth century. The Venetians and their allies defended religious skepticism (even atheism), scientific experimentation, sexual liberty (even pederasty), women's rights to an education and freedom from parental tyranny, the presence of women on the stage, and the seductive power of the female voice in opera.

The culture wars in Padua and Venice were an episode in what the late William J. Bouwsma called the waning of the Renaissance. From about 1550 to 1640 the cultural world of Europe was "full of contradictions," its thinkers constituted a "community of ambivalence," and the creative freedom characteristic of the early Renaissance "was constantly shadowed by doubt and anxiety."[1] Bouwsma argued that the hidden source of cultural change is anxiety, which in the case of the late Renaissance was produced by a surfeit of creative liberty that collapsed categories, blurred distinctions, and breached boundaries, the very bulwarks of cultural order that calm existential anxieties. By the late sixteenth century the creative freedom of the Renaissance had generated anxieties that had become unendurable for many. They sought to cope by erecting new forms of order. The culture wars resulted from the tension between the desire for liberation and the need for order, between those who explored the limits of cultural tolerance under the protection of Venice and those, mostly outside Venice, who abhorred the emotional, intellectual, and spiritual anarchy that resulted from such tolerance.

One of the singular achievements of the early Renaissance had been to promote a new source of cultural unity throughout Europe in the form of humanism. All sides of the culture wars shared in the heritage of Renaissance humanism, particularly its emphasis on the historical appreciation of sources, a critical understanding of the thought of the ancients, the problems of imitating nature in science and the arts, the evocative capacity of language to persuade, and its fallible capacity to represent. Catholics and Protestants, Italian and northern European intellectuals struggled with the anxieties provoked by the Renaissance heritage, and despite the new Babel of vernacular publishing, European elites remained culturally unified enough to follow Italian, which remained, like Latin, a lingua franca. In the dominion of the European Republic of Letters, Venice held a singular position because what happened in this cosmopolitan, commercial city, the center of Italian publishing, soon became widely known. (Probably half of all the books printed in Italy in the sixteenth century came from Venice.) In Venice enterprising bookmen (the ancestors of modern journalists) gathered and disseminated the news of Europe and the Middle East. The very idea that novelties, or "the news," might be of widespread interest and value was a creation of sixteenth- and seventeenth-century publishers, mostly Venetian, who were eager for sales. Venice's only real competitor as the cultural and journalistic capital of Europe was Paris. Rome was too identified with papal politics and Spanish influence to compete with Venice in this respect. Venice's official university at Padua remained until the 1620s the most prestigious in Europe. English and German Protestants, Polish, Jewish, and other "nations" in the student body also made Padua a pan-European, not just a local Venetian, university. Even the famous Venetian Accademia degli Incogniti, the home of libertine thought and the principal patron of opera, was an international organization in which Venetians were a distinct minority, even though every important Venetian intellectual of the era was a member.

One of the most disturbing sources of late-Renaissance anxiety was the collapse of the traditional hierarchic notion of the human self. Ancient and medieval thought depicted reason as governing the lower faculties of the will, the passions, and the body. Renaissance thought did not so much promote "individualism" as it cut away the intellectual props that presented humanity as the embodiment of a single divine idea, thereby forcing a desperate search for identity in many. John Martin has argued that during the Renaissance, individuals formed their sense of selfhood through a difficult negotiation between inner promptings and outer social roles. Individuals during the Renaissance looked both inward for emotional sustenance and outward for social assurance, and the friction between the inner and outer selves could sharpen anxieties.[2] The fragmentation of the self seems to have been especially acute in Venice, where the collapse of aristocratic marriage structures led to the formation of what Virginia Cox has called the single self, most clearly manifest in the works of several women writers who argued for the moral and intellectual equality of women with men.[3] As a consequence of the fragmented understanding of the self, such thinkers as Montaigne became obsessed with what was then the new concept of human psychology, a term in fact coined in this period.[4] A crucial problem in the new psychology was to define the relation between the body and the soul, in particular to determine whether the soul died with the body or was immortal. With its tradition of Averröist readings of Aristotle, some members of the philosophy faculty at the University of Padua recurrently questioned the Christian doctrine of the immortality of the soul as unsound philosophically. Other hierarchies of the human self came into question. Once reason was dethroned, the passions were given a higher value, so that the heart could be understood as a greater force than the mind in determining human conduct. When the body itself slipped out of its long-despised position, the sexual drives of the lower body were liberated and thinkers were allowed to consider sex, independent of its role in reproduction, a worthy manifestation of nature. The Paduan philosopher Cesare Cremonini's personal motto, "Intus ut libet, foris ut moris est," does not quite translate to "If it feels good, do it," but it comes very close. The collapse of the hierarchies of human psychology even altered the understanding of the human senses. The sense of sight lost its primacy as the superior faculty, the source of "enlightenment"; the Venetian theorists of opera gave that place in the hierarchy to the sense of hearing, the faculty that most directly channeled sensory impressions to the heart and passions.

The skepticism bred by the contradictions of late-Renaissance culture and the terrible experiences of the religious wars left medieval epistemology and textual authority without an anchor. No longer did the Bible or Aristotle or any other ancient text or author seem to provide universal truths applicable to all ages. For many late-Renaissance thinkers the only useful guidance was to be found in the particularities and contingencies of history. Skepticism, especially about the capacity of philosophy and theology to uncover truth, fostered historical consciousness. By the late sixteenth and early seventeenth centuries Padua and Venice, the homes of Francesco Patrizi and Paolo Sarpi, respectively, ranked among the most prominent centers of skeptical historiography, in whose explanations God and Fortune were banished as agents of human events. Paduan and Venetian historians understood history as a process that could be explained in purely human terms. People created history and were to blame for the folly of events. As a result, historiography replaced philosophy and theology as the appropriate medium for examining ethics, and irony permeated the rhetoric of history. The pervasive skepticism of the time finally led to doubts about the very capacity of language to mirror reality, to represent things. Writers concentrated on creating marvels rather than on reflecting nature and as a result often favored superficial verbal effects for their own sake.

During the culture wars nothing stirred up intellectual anxiety more than the cosmological theories of Copernicus that Galileo embraced. Many thinkers, especially Jesuits, found Copernicanism compatible with Catholic doctrine, and Galileo was at first received with honor in Rome after publishing his new discoveries with the telescope; yet Galileo and Copernicanism soon came under suspicion. Galileo had in fact been under observation for alleged heresies years before he became a noted advocate of Copernicanism. The problem was that Galileo was known as a doubter, as someone who restlessly questioned received truths, even before he definitively removed the earth and therefore humanity from the center of the universe and questioned whether the Bible was the best guide to the cosmos. Reintroducing doubt as the grounding for rational thought was the most significant achievement of seventeenth-century philosophy, but the virtue of doubt was not just a technical tool for someone like Descartes but a condition of the times. For those with eyes to see and the will to understand, the cosmos could no longer be understood as human-centered and circumscribed by biblical description, a fact that left many people disoriented and untethered intellectually, spiritually, emotionally.

Bouwsma argued that late-Renaissance culture was "generally ambivalent," that the early modern period was for many both the best of times and the worst of times. He explained this ambivalence as an outgrowth of the very freedoms Renaissance culture had promoted; for this reason, someone like Galileo could both espouse the new science and dread its consequences.[5] The distress and anxiety generated by the erosion of traditional forms of order were especially manifest in discussions of gender roles, an issue that preoccupied the libertines and the librettists of early opera. Few of them enjoyed the benefits of marriage, with its traditional gender roles. Gender bending was especially common on the stage, where boys played female roles, or in opera with its castrati and cross-dressing female singers. During the seventeenth century comic, tragic, and musical theater (that is, opera) became the most popular art form, the principal window onto the anxieties and stresses of the age. Once skepticism had compromised the capacity of the arts to imitate nature, theatrical artists, set loose from traditional conventions, sought to innovate, to create something that had never been experienced before. The conditions that fostered Shakespeare and Cervantes also gave rise to the first operas. The very popularity of theater created an anti-theatrical reaction, perhaps most famously in England, where the Puritans closed the theaters. In Italy Catholic bishops denounced comic theater; indeed in Venice the Jesuits succeeded in closing down the comic theaters, which reopened only after expulsion of the Society of Jesus in 1606. The Jesuits themselves put on sacred theatricals in their schools, but they also became the most systematic critics of secular theater, including bawdy commedia dell'arte and serious opera.

It would be too simple to depict the culture wars of the late Renaissance as a straightforward struggle between freedom and order, innovation and tradition. For their part, the skeptics, libertines, and librettists were often a confused lot, debaters addicted to debate for its own sake, and writers who hid behind the mask of anonymity, who pretended to be blind, or who obscured their own meaning with circumlocutions and allegories that might not be worth the effort to unravel. Their opponents, particularly the Jesuits, were just as committed to learning and to understanding the implications of Aristotle for theology, of the new science for biblical authority, and of humanism for education. Their theaters and their schools rivaled those of the Venetians. And the Jesuits were serious thinkers, serious men committed to serious issues, something that cannot always be said of the libertines and the librettists, whose commitment to playfulness and exotica has limited their significance. It would be a mistake to see one side as more "modern," more forward-looking than the other. The two sides reveal parallel tendencies in Western culture that have reappeared time and again since. The culture wars of our own times are not peculiar to us. They have a distinguished past. What some today depict as rash innovations, ideas that go against the traditions of Western civilization, are in fact deep-rooted. The virtues and perils of doubt, the place of homosexuals and women in society, the consequences of the breakdown of marriage structures, and the power of the arts to stir sometimes disturbing emotions preoccupied the thinkers in the culture wars of the late Renaissance much as the same ideas still engage our attention today.

ONE

The Skeptics

GALILEO'S TELESCOPE
AND CREMONINI'S
HEADACHE

$\mathcal{B}$OTH a familiar and an unfamiliar story can be told about the friendly rivalry between Galileo Galilei and his colleague at the University of Padua, Cesare Cremonini, who was the second professor of Aristotelian philosophy. Both professors had been hired away from other universities during the 1590s, and at Padua they became two of the most celebrated thinkers of their day. The familiar story speaks across the centuries about the conflict between freedom of thought and the proofs of science, on the one hand, and the blindness of dogmatic allegiance to ancient philosophy on the other. Bertolt Brecht's play *The Life of Galileo* still captures best the mythopoeic dimension of the familiar story. In an early scene, the curator at the University of Padua explains to Galileo why he will not receive a raise in salary:

You should not altogether forget that, while the Republic [of Venice] may not pay as much as certain Princes do, it guarantees freedom of research. We in Padua admit even Protestants to our lectures! And we grant them doctorates. Not only did we not surrender Signor Cremonini to the Inquisition when it was proved to us—*proved*, Signor Galilei— that he gave vent to irreligious utterances, but we even voted him a higher salary. As far away as Holland it is known that Venice is the republic where the Inquisition has no say. And that is worth something to you who are an astronomer— that is, devoting yourself to a science which has for a considerable time ceased to show a due respect for the teachings of the Church![1]

Later in the play Brecht invents a scene at the court of the grand duke of Tuscany in which Galileo attempts to persuade Grand Duke Cosimo II to look through the telescope. Present in the scene are characters called the Mathematician and the Philosopher, the latter often understood as a stand-in for Cremonini. When invited to look into the telescope, the Philosopher objects, "I fear that things are not quite as simple as all that. Signor Galilei, before we apply ourselves to your famous instrument we would like to have the pleasure of a disputation. The theme: Can such planets [that is, the moons of Jupiter, called the Medicean stars] exist?" Galileo: "I thought you could simply look through the telescope and convince yourselves." The Mathematician and the Philosopher continue to cite the authority of "the cosmos of the divine Aristotle," to argue that no such planets can possibly exist and even to suggest that the Medicean stars had been painted on the lens of the telescope. In the end, the Grand Duke and his entourage, including the Mathematician and the Philosopher, leave for a court ball without ever bothering to peer into Galileo's glass.[2] Dogmatism and indifference blind them to facts evident to anyone willing to look.

Brecht's fictional debate in the court of the grand duke was suggested by an actual episode in the relationship between Galileo and Cremonini. In a letter to Galileo dated shortly after the publication in 1610 of the *Starry Messenger (Sidereus Nuncius)*, which announced the new telescope discoveries, Paolo Gualdo reported a conversation he had had with Cremonini regarding the telescope and the philosopher's own forthcoming publication on the celestial controversies, *Disputation on the Heavens (Disputatio de coelo*, 1613). Gualdo wrote that he had said jokingly to Cremonini, "Signor Galilei is waiting anxiously for the appearance of your new work."

Cremonini: "He has no reason to fear, because I don't make any reference to his observations."

Gualdo: "It will be enough that you take the completely opposite position to his."

"Oh, yes," Cremonini replied, "I don't want to approve of things which I neither have any knowledge about nor have seen."

"This is," Gualdo said, "what has displeased Sig. Galilei, that you have not wanted to see it."

Cremonini: "I believe that there are others who have not looked, and moreover to observe through those glasses gives me a headache. That's enough. I don't want to know anything more about it."

Gualdo: "Sir, there is sense in the saying of the masters; it's good to follow sacred antiquity."

Later Cremonini burst out, "Oh how much better it would be for Sig. Galilei not to go down this path, and not leave the liberty of Padua!"[3]

Here are all the elements of the famous narrative that has had such significance for our culture: freedom for scientific experimentation guaranteed by the protection the Republic of Venice extended to its professors at the University of Padua; the refusal of hidebound philosophers even to acknowledge new sensory evidence; and the warnings about the dangers that lay ahead for Galileo if he left Padua. Of course, it is well known that by later joining the court of the grand duke of Tuscany, Galileo made himself vulnerable to prosecution by the Roman Inquisition, which would eventually silence him and intimidate many other scientists in the Catholic world. To borrow an anachronistic label from our own time, Galileo and his opponents were the principal antagonists in the culture wars of the late Renaissance, wars that pitted experimental science against blind adherence to the theories of Aristotle and religious dogmatism. Embedded in this narrative is a presage of the triumph of scientific reason. The story is so meaningful because we think we know that over the long term science will win out over Aristotle and the theologians through its superior explanatory power with regard to natural phenomena.

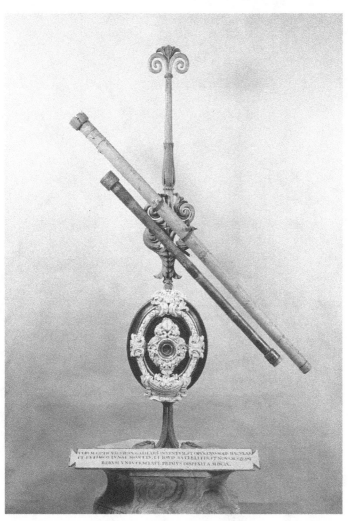

The telescope and lens of Galileo Galilei.

Side by side with this version, however, exists an unfamiliar story about Galileo and Cremonini, one made possible by discoveries in the newly opened archives of the Holy Office in Rome and by the recent reappraisals of Cremonini's thought. If one follows a trajectory starting with Cremonini's career rather than with Galileo's, a rather different version of the culture wars of the period emerges, along with a trend in thought that was far more subversive of Christian doctrine than Galileo's Copernicanism. The most significant culture wars of the late Renaissance derive from Cremonini's religious skepticism and the libertine legacy passed along to his many students who directly challenged the authority of the post-Tridentine Church. In Padua during the forty-year period between 1591 and Cremonini's death in 1631, clear lines of cultural and institutional conflict were drawn between a faction of the faculty at Padua in which Galileo and Cremonini were close allies and the Jesuit fathers who attempted to establish an alternative college in the city. The most serious antagonists in the culture wars were Cremonini and the Jesuit fathers, and it seems that Galileo's troubles with the Roman Inquisition began because of his association with Cremonini.

At stake were competing philosophies of pedagogy and concerted attempts to influence the youth from the ruling classes. The alliance between Galileo and Cremonini was more than one of mutual antagonism to the Jesuits. Whatever their intellectual differences, they shared a profound skepticism about both received knowledge and the certainty of any claims to absolute truth. They sought open-ended methods of investigation and practiced a style of intellectual inquiry that sometimes led them to mask their most unconventional views.

Intellectual dissimulation, masking of meaning, and pretended blindness, as symbolized by Cremonini's refusal to look into Galileo's telescope, became the hallmark of a whole generation of intellectuals. This was especially true of Cremonini's students, who in 1630 founded in Venice the Accademia degli Incogniti (Academy of the Unknowns), which openly espoused religious skepticism and libertine morality. One of the most intriguing aspects of the enormous cultural output of the Incogniti was their debates about gender roles, which included a series of exchanges between Suor Arcangela Tarabotti, the most vocal critic of forced monasticism and paternal tyranny, and Ferrante Pallavicino, the misogynist enfant terrible of the Incogniti. Pallavicino, like Galileo, made the mistake of leaving the protective embrace of the Venetian republic, thus becoming the martyr among the Incogniti. From the Incogniti a direct line can be drawn to the French Enlightenment thinkers and to debates about the status of women in the Republic of Letters. After 1637 members of the Incogniti began to write libretti and helped sponsor the remarkable flowering of the new art form of opera. It stands to reason that the Incogniti, as victims of the restrictive marriage practices of the Venetian patriciate—according to which only a few members of each generation were allowed to marry, women were forced into convents, and men were driven to resort to relationships with concubines and courtesans—would transform the opera stage into the reflection of a society of masquerade, in which circumscribed sexual and social roles made everyone hide behind a mask of polite manners. In the opera house spectators were often literally unknown, since most members of the audience, especially women, arrived wearing a real mask. As we shall see, the musical theories about polyphony and monody of Galileo's father, Vincenzo, and the libertine views of Cremonini, laid the groundwork for the inventors of commercial opera.

After teaching at Ferrara for thirteen years, Cremonini took up the second chair in natural philosophy at Padua in 1591, the year before Galileo arrived as professor of mathematics.[4] By the end of the sixteenth century, Padua had indisputably become the premier university in Italy, and probably in all of Europe, largely because of consistent protection and support from the Venetian government. Because Padua paid significantly higher faculty salaries, it had the largest budget of any Italian university, even though the Padua faculty was about half the size of Bologna's. Padua was the only Italian university to prevent corrupting favoritism by passing legislation that limited the number of Paduans and barred Venetian patricians and citizens from professorships. (Bologna, by contrast, reserved the ordinary professorships for citizens who were Bolognese by birth.) As a result of these policies, Padua rose to true distinction. By the 1530s it boasted the best medical faculty in Europe "by a wide margin": it had the first professor of botany or pharmacology anywhere, the first botanical garden, and the first clinical facility. The local government accommodated the university in extraordinary ways, such as timing executions to fit into Vesalius's dissection schedule. Vesalius and Falloppio even encouraged their students to steal bodies for dissection from funerals and graves, while the authorities looked the other way. In fact, the public interest in the university was such that dissections became a form of theater performed during carnival season for local citizens who appeared in masks.[5] The faculties of law and philosophy were also distinguished. Far more than the state university of the Republic of Venice, Padua was, despite its modest size, thoroughly international in its scope and influence.[6]

During the late sixteenth century, however, the university started to face serious competition from the local Jesuit college. One of the earliest houses of the Society of Jesus had been founded in Padua in 1542, and it gradually expanded to accept non-Jesuit students and enhanced its curriculum beyond the preuniversity-level Latin humanistic schooling that was the focus of Jesuit pedagogy. By 1589, the college had 450 students, including 70 nobles, and had added a three-year philosophical curriculum that paralleled the lectures offered at the university. In this expansion the Society had been supported by many Paduan and Venetian families, concerned by the spiritual poverty and moral decline of the university, which had been cast in the worst possible light in the Jesuits' sermons. These families voluntarily sent their sons to a safer environment, where they thought the boys would receive considerably more attention from their teachers than ever was offered at the university. The Jesuit reforms were a direct challenge to the negligent and lazy habits of the university students, known as the Bovisti (from the Palazzo Bo where they took lectures), who regularly sent their servants or paid substitutes to attend lectures and take exams. Competition from the Jesuit college directly threatened the status quo among university students and also among faculty members, who were forced to increase their teaching loads by offering private tutoring and extra lectures. With the deaths in 1589 of two professors, Giacomo Zabarella and Girolamo Capizucchio, the Jesuits lost their most influential friends on the faculty. When the Jesuits began to ring a bell to announce the start of classes and to offer doctoral degrees, their tense relationship with the university snapped.[7]

During the spring of 1591, graffiti attacking the Jesuits appeared on the walls of their college, and then in July on two successive days Bovisti students surrounding the Jesuit college shot off guns, smashed windows, and painted more anti-Jesuit graffiti. On July 12, a group of university students, including young Venetian patricians from prominent families, stripped off their clothes, dressed themselves in sheets, and marched on the Jesuit college, flashing women and children along the way. Once inside the college, they threw off the sheets and ran about naked, shouting obscenities at the Jesuit fathers and the younger students. The ringleaders of this adolescent prank faced heavy fines, but the incident actually increased hostility toward the Jesuits in Padua.

A student delegation traveled to Venice to speak to the

Senate against the Jesuit college, but when the disorders continued, the rectors of the university decided to act and sent a faculty delegation, headed by the first and second professors of natural philosophy, Francesco Piccolomini and Cesare Cremonini, to appeal directly to the doge. Cremonini took the lead in defending the anti-Jesuit students, by delivering a passionate, polemical oration that was full of exaggerations and inaccuracies but that brought results. Cremonini invoked the distinguished tradition of the university, which had first received a charter from the *stupor mundi*, Emperor Frederick II. Venice had confirmed the charter in 1405. The university community, however, was now divided, because the Jesuits had established an "antistudio" in Padua that stole students from the Bo, which by Venetian law had exclusive rights to higher education in the Venetian republic. Cremonini appealed to Venetian patriotism by noting that the Jesuits had opened their studio without the permission of the Venetian Senate but with some seals granted by foreigners, by which he clearly meant the popes. He noted that it was an illicit university because it had published a course schedule that listed faculty members teaching specific classes at defined hours and had rung a bell to announce the classes. Feeding fears of sedition, Cremonini argued that the Jesuits had provoked riots and divided the students "into factions, some calling themselves the Jesuits, others the Bovisti, just like the Guelfs and Ghibellines." After three days of heated debate and divided votes, the Senate responded by blaming the Jesuits for the recent events and ordered them to restrict the audi-

ence for their teaching to Jesuit novices, in order not to con-
travene the statutes of the public university. Attempts were
made in later years to repeal the prohibition, but after the Jesuits were banished from the entire Venetian dominion between 1606 and 1657, the point was moot.[8]

Although sixty senators abstained from voting against the
Jesuits, an indication of significant political anxiety about attacking the Society, the fathers were not invited to respond to
Cremonini's attack. Cremonini's oration, however, required
some answer, especially because a published version was soon
circulating in anti-Jesuit circles throughout Europe, and nota-
bly in civil-war-torn Paris, where it was not yet clear whether
Henry of Navarre would be able to bring the religious wars
to an end. Five apologies penned by prominent Jesuits began
to circulate among sympathetic Venetians. The Jesuits returned the Paduan philosopher's vitriol in kind: Cremonini,
the fathers said, was a "man . . . more habituated to carrying
a scimitar at his side and a harquebus on his shoulder than
Aristotle to his university chair, and much better at handling
arms and at fighting a campaign than at lecturing from the
university chair of public studies." Cremonini was "a stipen-
diary philosopher," a "mercenary philosopher . . ., pulled
from the mud and reeds of the swamps of Ferrara, who
knows how to interfere with God, and even for a few florins
serves up barbarian concepts and a dull tongue to the Bo of
Padua." He was further accused of being a "stinking spider"
that sucked out all the good doctrine and spat into the ears
of his students only "pestilential venom."[9]

Behind the screen of mutual insults lay real doctrinal and pedagogical differences. It was not the modernist breakthrough that pitted the Jesuits against Cremonini and Galileo—not the scientific explanations for material phenomena—but rather the issue of the proper relationship between theology and philosophy in intellectual inquiry. Many Jesuits, of course, had their own scientific interests, but in Padua they objected to Cremonini's teaching of "the errors of Aristotle and other philosophers." Citing Leo X's decretal from the Fifth Lateran Council of 1513, which had been made necessary by the teachings of the Paduan philosopher Pietro Pomponazzi, the Jesuits objected to Cremonini's apparent denial of the immortality of the soul. To teach philosophy to students who were not grounded in theology was dangerous, because philosophy should be ancillary to theology. Misuse of philosophy was, in fact, the result of a larger institutional problem at the university because, as the most vociferous of the Jesuit apologists, Paolo Comitoli, wrote, all students must serve the Catholic religion and "thus, by necessity all public education must be principally anchored in the ecclesiastical and pontifical authority, not in ducal, royal, imperial, or whatever-you-want republican authority."[10] Since the lay teachers had refused any supervision from the proper religious teachers and accepted only the authority of the Senate of Venice, the professors had allowed heresy to flourish at the university and had even protected the German and Polish students, many of whom were Lutheran or Calvinist agitators against the Jesuits. In fact, despite the Tridentine decrees that required otherwise, Protestant students at Padua were not required to make a profession of faith to receive the doctorate.[11]

These polemical objections from the soldiers of Catholicism may seem predictable, but their disputes with the university professors had as much to do with pedagogy as with privileging theology over philosophy. The principal inspiration for Jesuit pedagogy, in fact, came from the disappointing experiences at the University of Padua that Juan Alfonso de Polanco (secretary for Ignatius of Loyola and for the subsequent two generals of the Society) and some other early Jesuits had had while enrolled there. Polanco had found that the instruction lacked structure and drill, and consequently any means for accumulating skills. By combining the pedagogy of the Brethren of the Common Life with the system used at the University of Paris, which divided students into graded classes, gave responsibility for each class to a single instructor, and required a strict daily schedule, the Jesuits created an exacting curriculum of lectures, drills, and disputations geared to the age and competence of the students. Jesuit teachers provided their charges with considerable individual attention that helped students make progress through each stage of learning. Jesuits accepted the humanists' proposition that the mastery of classical Greek and Latin language and literature inculcated virtue and helped foster Christian piety.

Considerable emphasis was placed on teaching upright behavior, so that the classrooms were quiet and disciplined. The Jesuits concerned themselves with the whole student, providing not just for formal educational needs but for recreation and sports. Students were required to attend Mass frequently, to participate in the liturgical hours, and to engage in daily examination of conscience and regular confession. Perhaps most innovative was the Jesuit emphasis on theater, in which music and dance became an integral part of the performance. As John O'Malley put it, "the significance of theater in all its aspects for Jesuit colleges can hardly be overestimated."[12] The proper role of theater became one of the battlegrounds in the culture wars of the seventeenth century, in which Venetian grand opera would serve as a foil to Jesuit theater.

Perhaps the most irreconcilable disagreement between the Jesuits and the Paduan philosophers involved the teaching of Aristotle. The Jesuits modeled their views of Aristotle on the Scholastic and specifically Thomistic theology of Paris, but they developed a distinctly Jesuit way of proceeding. Rather than lecturing on Aristotelian philosophy directly from the text, glossed by the professor's commentaries, the Jesuits relied on textbooks that systematically followed arguments from fundamental principles. Such an approach allowed them to demonstrate that rigorous arguments based on Aristotle's philosophy led to conclusions that were in perfect conformity with Christianity. The Jesuit method was specifically designed to counter readings of Aristotle that were characteristic of the Paduan tradition going back to Pomponazzi, who had argued that either the first principles of Aristotle yielded results contrary to Christian faith, or at least those principles could not be employed to prove Christian dogmas, most famously the immortality of the soul. In opposition to the Paduan Aristotelians, the Jesuits created logical, even original, arguments that preserved the Scholastic enterprise to reconcile Aristotle with revealed Christianity. To their way of thinking, Aristotle proved that the rational soul is in fact immortal.[13] Whatever other differences with the Jesuits the Paduan philosophers (and especially Cremonini) had, it is hard to imagine their tolerating a direct assault right in their own city on everything they stood for. For their part the Jesuits certainly recognized that Padua was perhaps the most important intellectual battleground in the Catholic world, the place where heterodox views flourished most openly.

The Jesuit college in Padua, therefore, presented a real challenge to the university, especially because, whatever the philosophical debates, many parents thought the Society provided a superior education. The Jesuits offered a complete cycle of studies, a broader curriculum than that available at the Faculty of Arts, free tuition, systematic didactic methods, and individual attention to the students. Whereas the professors in the Faculty of Arts at the university delivered between sixty and seventy lectures per year, at the Jesuit college each instructor gave three hundred, in addition to the time spent on daily repetition and organized monthly debates. The only way for a university student to receive the kind of attention the Jesuits offered for free was to pay his professors for private tutoring. Paul Grendler has argued that private teaching at the university had a particularly corrosive effect on the lectures, which the students skipped or despised. As the Jesuit critic Giovan Domenico Bonaccorsi reported, at the Bo, "very frequently the chatter, shouts, whistles, and banging on the broken and damaged desks [make so much noise] that for whole periods whatever leaves the mouth of the doctor disappears into the air and never reaches the ears of the students."[14] In this chaos the serious students retreated to the privacy of their professors' houses for personal instruction. Private teaching became very popular, both because those students who could afford it wanted it and because the professors found it profitable. Until 1606 Galileo earned 44 percent more from private teaching than from his university salary. Besides offering the entire mathematical curriculum on a private basis, Galileo sold a didactic package to students that consisted of a compass, training in its use, and an instruction booklet. Galileo received only an average salary and did not have many students, but Cremonini was probably the best-paid professor in Italy and was so popular that he ran an extensive program of private instruction for hundreds of students. According to the report of his students, Cremonini did not abuse the system and was a charismatic inspiration to them. Other instructors were less responsible. Because of private teaching, some students were able to avoid the five-to-seven-year residence requirement at the university and took their degrees after only a year or two of private drilling on brief passages from the required texts for examination. Since professors also collected fees for examinations, it was in their interest to rush as many students as possible through to the degree. These were the abuses for which the Jesuits promised a remedy.[15]

The loyalty of the future generations was at stake. Jesuits were distrusted because they put loyalty to the Society and the pope above all else. As the anti-Jesuit Servite friar Paolo Sarpi put it, "The Jesuit Schools have never graduated a son obedient to his father, devoted to his fatherland, and loyal to his prince."[16] The protection the Venetian Senate gave the university certainly had a lot to do with old school ties, but in addition the university professors could be controlled in a way the Jesuit fathers never could. Venetian patricians who had received a Jesuit education remained defenders of the Society, but they were persistently outvoted. In 1612 the Senate prohibited any Venetian subject from sending children, relatives, or dependents to study at a Jesuit college outside Venetian territory.[17] Within the small compass of Padua a battle of European significance was being fought, especially because of the prestige of the university and the large number of foreign students in attendance there. That battle has often been misunderstood as one between science and religion. Galileo's materialism and Copernicanism were far less significant than the disputes about pedagogy, and the serious challenge to orthodoxy came less from Galileo's science than from the readings of Aristotle by that "mercenary philosopher" Cesare Cremonini.

The pedagogical battles in Padua during Cremonini's tenure took place in a climate of growing tension between

Venice and Rome, especially after the 1580s, when the Jesuit influence over some patrician families became evident. Besides establishing various charitable institutions in Venice and the college in Padua, the Jesuits had influenced governmental policy, including the suppression of Venetian commedia dell'arte theaters. Disputes over church ownership of land, which amounted to a quarter of all the territory in the Venetian state, and over Venice's attempts to try priests for major crimes in civil courts heightened the tension, which culminated in the bull of interdict against Venice delivered on Christmas Day 1605. The bill of particulars against Venice included the suppression of the Jesuit college in Padua and toleration of the teaching of heretical ideas at the university. The Venetian Senate responded by refusing to publish or enforce the interdict and by appointing Fra Paolo Sarpi official consultant in theology and canon law to help defend the government against the pope. Sarpi's skepticism and empirical approach in his writings on behalf of Venice have been thoroughly analyzed by William Bouwsma, David Wootton, and Vittorio Frajese.[18] Sarpi confronted all the principal issues of his day, not the least of which was Jesuit education, of which he was perhaps the most perceptive critic. Sarpi rejected the commonly held opinion that the Jesuits had developed the best education system. To Sarpi's mind,

> education is not an absolute thing which has grades of perfection, of which the Jesuit Fathers have attained the highest,

but education is relative to government. Therefore youth is educated in such a way that what is good and useful for one government is harmful for another, and education received variety according to the variety of governments. What is useful for a military state, which is maintained and increased with violence, is pernicious to a peaceful one, which is conserved through the observance of laws.[19]

According to Sarpi, the Jesuits subordinated all aspects of the curriculum to the ecclesiastical ideal of government. Sarpi's relating of teaching methods to the form of government struck at the very heart of Jesuit pedagogy, which did not allow young minds to grow through doubt or by comparison of alternate systems of thought. In Sarpi's view, the Jesuits answered far too many questions with too much certainty.[20]

Sarpi's well-known polemics owed a great deal to Cremonini and the Paduan tradition of philosophical skepticism. Cremonini's influence made itself directly felt in other settings, outside the university. Along with twenty-six prominent Venetian and Paduan aristocrats and churchmen, Cremonini and Galileo were cofounders in 1599 of the Accademia dei Ricoverati, which actively engaged in discussions of religion and morality. The Ricoverati became a model for two other academies, the Incoronati in Padua and the Incogniti in Venice, both of which registered Cremonini's influence. These academies offered distinctive venues for free debate, unencumbered by university rules and procedures, and the Ricoverati was so open that it brought Cremonini and his allies together in debate with their old antagonists, the Jesuits and their supporters. The contradictory impulses created by such openness, however, brought the Ricoverati academy to the verge of collapse a mere decade after its founding. Through the publication of moral tracts and novels in the vernacular, the Incogniti, founded by Cremonini's students, furthered Cremonini's philosophical ideas on a much larger scale than had the Ricoverati, in addressing only the small world of Latin-reading philosophers. Another arena of Cremonini's influence was the nation of German students of which he served as the protector for thirty-nine years. The German-speaking students in philosophy, medicine, and theology, the largest association at the university, organized a range of activities. Thus, Cremonini was always in close contact with Protestant students. Those from Ingolstadt and Prague, where the Jesuits under the protection of local princes exercised a strong influence, were particularly hostile to the Society. Probably at the instigation of the famous Jesuit thinker Antonio Possevino, Pope Gregory XIV asked the Holy Office to investigate the Protestant students at Padua. In Padua the Jesuits had even tried to recruit German-speaking priests, to sort out the good Catholics from the heretics among the students, but the attempt merely created more hostility.[21]

Cremonini's and Galileo's membership in the Ricoverati provides a clue to an intellectual affinity between them that went deeper than their alliance in university politics. It has long been thought that Galileo's troubles with the Holy Office began after the publication in 1610 of the *Starry Messenger* because of its Copernicanism, which led to the condemnation of Copernican theory in 1616 and ultimately to Galileo's trial in 1633 for failure to respect the 1616 injunction.[22] However, recent research in the Inquisition archives in Venice and especially in the newly opened archives of the Congregation of the Holy Inquisition reveals that the Holy Office considered both Cremonini and Galileo to be persons of interest and subjects of investigation long before 1610, and for reasons that had nothing to do with Copernicanism. In fact, over a thirty-year period beginning in 1598, more than eighty Inquisition files were opened on Cremonini, making him one of the most, if not the most, thoroughly investigated thinkers in the early modern Catholic world.[23] Certainly, only the protection of Venice kept him from suffering Galileo's fate or worse.

In 1604 Cremonini and Galileo were jointly denounced before the Paduan tribunal as heretics and consummate libertines. The indictment refers to an investigation of Galileo by the Inquisition in Florence before his transfer to Padua in 1592, an indication that Galileo's troubles with the Church went back to his early career. The 1604 denunciation alleged that Galileo was practicing astrology and arguing that the stars controlled, as opposed to influenced, all human actions.[24] Cremonini's error lay in his failure to take account of the immortality of the soul when explaining Aristotle to his students. The accusation originated with a sermon preached during Lent in the Padua cathedral. A Jesuit father had thundered from the pulpit that all good Catholics had an obligation of conscience to report the heretical opinions about the mortality of the soul that were circulating in the city, in particular at the university. Everyone recognized that he was talking about Cremonini, and many assumed that the sermon was an act of revenge for Cremonini's infamous oration to the Venetian Senate in 1591 against the Jesuit college. Whether moved by the sermon or by other, less pious motives, some of the faithful incriminated the two professors.

During the inquisitorial proceedings, Cremonini's arch-rival at the university, Camillo Belloni, declared that although it caused him great distress, he was impelled by his conscience to tell the truth about Cremonini. Part of the truth he did not tell was that Cremonini was both more popular with the students and much better paid, and that he enjoyed the full protection of the Venetian authorities. Belloni in his deposition accused Cremonini of holding the Christological heresy, which rejected the incarnation of Christ and his death on the cross. Cremonini had supposedly confessed to the heresy six or seven years before, to a third party. Although Belloni had never personally heard Cremonini deny the immortality of the soul, his views were common knowledge about town, and the students who frequented his private seminars openly discussed them, along with other impieties, and repeated them in exams. "Everybody knows that Cremonini holds that the soul is mortal, not only because of Aristotle but in its very nature."[25]

Galileo's principal accuser was none other than his own amanuensis, Silvestro Piagnoni, who had copied the workbooks that Galileo sold to his students. After eighteen months' residence in Galileo's house, Piagnoni had been forced to leave because of debts. Piagnoni knew a great deal about the comings and goings in Galileo's house and had heard from Galileo's mother that the Florentine had some terrible secrets from his youth that only the family knew about. Piagnoni was indiscrete enough to say that Galileo never went to Mass or took the sacraments, that he kept a lover in a nearby house, and that he read unedifying books. Piagnoni further reported that Galileo cast nativity horoscopes for many people and that Galileo insisted his clients "should accept his judgment as solid and not doubt that they must follow his advice exactly." But in the end Piagnoni backed off from the heretical implications of these revelations and asserted that "on matters of faith I believe that he believes." The most revealing piece of information, however, was incidental to the charges. When asked who Galileo associated with, Piagnoni replied, "He is with Cremonini practically every day."[26]

The Paduan inquisitor was a Franciscan, Cesare Lippi, who was also the professor of metaphysics *in via Scoti* at the Faculty of Arts and a colleague of the two accused professors. He shared with Galileo an interest in mathematics and astronomy; indeed, a few months after the denunciation Lippi collaborated with him on measuring the supernova that appeared on October 9, 1604. Lippi attempted to quash the whole business in Padua and managed to keep Rome ignorant of the allegations against Galileo, but Rome insisted that the trial against Cremonini go ahead because he had already been tried in 1599 for reviving Pomponazzi's heresy on the mortality of the soul and must therefore be considered a relapsed heretic. The Venetian government, whose representatives considered the attack on one of its professors an affair of state, attempted to get the matter dropped, on the grounds that Cremonini was the victim of obvious personal animosity. Ignoring the ecclesiastical tribunal, Cremonini, with characteristic aplomb, addressed the Venetian Senate in his own defense. After apologizing for any embarrassment he may have caused his Venetian patrons, he painted the entire matter as an assault on his honor—not just his personal honor but the honor bestowed on him as a public man serving the Venetian republic. He claimed to be always observant regarding religious matters, both as a Christian and as a philosopher, because it is alien to philosophy to destroy religion. If he had transgressed, as his accusers claimed, then he had transgressed against the chair he held in Padua and would voluntarily submit to punishment according to Venetian laws. The divisions in the Senate revealed deep fissures within the patriciate, but after a motion passed to send a letter to the Inquisition on Cremonini's behalf, the immediate danger faded for him.[27]

The inquisitors nevertheless remained vigilant, and new denunciations of Cremonini arrived with regularity in 1607, 1608, 1609, and 1611. In 1613, when Cremonini sought to publish his own argument about the challenge by Copernicus to Aristotelian cosmology, the same *Disputation on the Heavens* that offended his friend Galileo by ignoring the evidence visible through the telescope, he wisely obtained prepublica-

Portrait of Galileo by Ottavio Leoni, chalk drawing.

tion approval from the Paduan inquisitors and the secretary of the Senate. However, once the prelates of the Roman congregation had an opportunity to review the published text, they found even more reason to object to it than to Galileo's *Starry Messenger*. The *Disputation on the Heavens* is a reactionary work that attacks all presumed knowledge since Aristotle— not just Copernicus but Ptolemy as well—and its hallmark is an insistence on the necessity of systematic reason. Cremonini considered philosophy a method without guarantees of truth, so even on the points where he agreed with Christian doctrines, he refused to assume they were valid philosophically. Philosophy was capable only of laying out a range of possible truths. Cremonini revealed himself to be both a rigorous rationalist in the Aristotelian mode and a philosophical skeptic—patterns in his style of thought that were not lost on the defenders of orthodoxy. The Roman congregation sent the Paduan inquisitor a list of objections, to which Cremonini replied. Rome argued that Cremonini's interpretation of Aristotle did not conform to Christian truth. Cremonini insisted that philosophy and theology be kept separate and refused to correct his text, which he said was the job of a theologian, not a philosopher. The two sides went back and forth with Cremonini stating that he did not object if the Inquisition had a theologian correct his text, but as a philosopher he could only teach and write what could be demonstrated philosophically and nothing more. He was paid to teach Aristotle, and if he did anything else, he would be obliged to return his salary, for he would not be performing the duties for which he was hired. The congregation put the book on the Index of Prohibited Books but was unable to penetrate the protective shield the Venetian Senate provided for Cremonini. Nevertheless, harassment continued. The case was reopened in 1625, and after his death in 1631 the Holy Office concluded that Cremonini's books contained erroneous propositions that were absolutely heretical because of Cremonini's own ideas, rather than because of his misreading of Aristotle.[28]

The persistent investigation and systematic persecution of Cremonini certainly exceeded the Inquisition's interest in Galileo during the same period, but the Cremonini affair lacks the dramatic outcome of Galileo's trial simply because the philosopher was never foolish enough to leave Padua. The Cremonini case, however, suggests some important reinterpretations of the investigation of Galileo by the Church. The idea that the inquisitors investigated Galileo because of his opposition to Aristotle now seems untenable. Pope Urban VIII was known as an anti-Aristotelian. Galileo offended Urban because the pope's own words were put into the mouth of Simplicio in the *Dialogue Concerning the Two Chief World Systems* (1632), and it must have especially galled Urban to be depicted as an Aristotelian. Had Galileo made Simplicio more obviously a stand-in for his old friend Cremonini, Galileo would probably have avoided the pope's wrath. And then Galileo always claimed that he was himself an Aristotelian. But what if he was the kind of Aristotelian who shared Cremonini's views about the plurality of modes of inquiry

This engraving from the collected works of Galileo Galilei depicts him presenting his telescope to the Muses. He points to the heavens, where the moons of Jupiter, which he named the Medicean stars, are represented in the form of the arms of the Medici family, Galileo's patrons after he left Padua. From *Opere di Galileo Galilei* (Bologna, 1655–1656).

and Cremonini's skepticism about the ability of any of these methods to discover absolute truth? The most astute modern reader of Cremonini, Heinrich C. Kuhn, has even argued that Galileo can best be understood "as a reader of Cremonini," a proposition at least partially confirmed by the marginal notations in some of Cremonini's books known to have been owned by Galileo.[29] These considerations raise the question of what Cremonini actually thought, as opposed to what his enemies said he thought.

Answering that question is not a simple task. The problem comes from trying to peak behind Cremonini's many masks. As Kuhn puts it, these philosophical masks enabled Cremonini to take on a persona, and "this role is frequently a disquieting one that makes Cremonini an uncomfortable philosopher, uncomfortable for more than three and a half centuries, uncomfortable still today."[30] His favorite masquerade, that of the blind man, was the one he was playing when he refused to peer into Galileo's telescope. His refusal to see what was before his very eyes created the lasting impression embodied in Brecht's character of the Philosopher—he was "insignificant as a philosopher," the author of "pedantic discussions," the "last scholastic," and "the boring philosopher."[31] Nevertheless, his contemporaries, including his enthusiastic students, his jealous colleagues, and even his theological critics, considered him an important thinker, a genius who had to be taken seriously or silenced. Were they merely deceived by his undeniable personal charisma, or does he deserve more credit than he has been given? Cremonini was the highest-paid philosopher in Italy. He could draw more than four hundred students to his lectures. He was on William Harvey's examination committee for the M.D. degree. He was the patron of the "Polish Paduans," including the "Polish Pascal," Jan Brozek, the great Euclidian who was inspired by Cremonini's "humanity, humility, and gentleness." Leibniz cited him as a forerunner, someone who had anticipated his own skeptical position.[32] Many contemporaries considered Cremonini a far more significant thinker than Galileo.

The best approach would be to look at Cremonini's own writings. His *Treatise on Paedia* (*Tractatus de Paedia*, 1596) follows the tradition of the Paduan Aristotelians, Pietro Pomponazzi and Cremonini's immediate predecessor, Giacomo Zabarella. What was at stake for Cremonini was clear in the debates of the previous generation of Paduan philosophers, including Francesco Piccolomini and Zabarella. As John Herman Randall, Jr. elegantly explained, "against [Piccolomini's] demand that metaphysics must furnish the starting-point and the frame of reference in all science, and that the scientist must imitate the fixed structure of nature, Zabarella maintains the independence and self-sufficiency of natural science, and indeed of each particular subject-matter, making the end of knowledge and inquiry a human thing, and directing the sciences toward human goals and aims."[33] Cremonini likewise asserted the primacy of human experience as the source of all knowledge but went even further than Zabarella in his definition of *paedia*. He did not follow the Greek interpretation of *paedia* as the forms of life characteristic of a people, something akin to what we might mean by culture in the anthropological sense; rather, he considered that *paedia* is derived from experience itself. *Paedia* is the power to judge rightly through the application of logic to experience, and it is always a conscious operation, not just habitual. Cremonini turned the problem into one of method: "Although one may be instructed by ingenuity or by logic, unless he has also experienced the thing he is to judge, he will not be able to exercise judgment." These are the grounds on which he disagreed with Galileo's mathematics, which proceeded by induction from the observation of material phenomena. Cremonini insisted that the most fruitful method involved more than the ascent to abstract causes that could be represented mathematically. One must pay systematic attention to the effects of phenomena. He applied this approach as much to the natural sciences as to ethics or theology. By advocating close analysis of experience, he refocused attention on the methods of discovery, which would include the phases of both induction and demonstration after the fact.[34]

Characteristic of Cremonini was the way he turned his philosophical interests toward pedagogy by making the student-teacher relationship the core of his philosophy of inquiry. Unlike the Jesuits' pedagogy, which emphasized student discipline and systematic, step-by-step learning through an approved course of instruction, Cremonini described the student-teacher relationship as reciprocal, and the best method of instruction as Socratic. As he put it, the artist can work with whatever material is at hand, but the philosopher cannot teach just anyone, but rather can teach only those students who are predisposed by nature and experience to understand his lessons. He contrasted predisposition with discipline-induced docility, which might allow the student to hear but not to understand. True predisposition enables the listener to absorb the principles behind a specific lesson and to live them his whole life. One of Cremonini's examples of predisposition reveals why he was so popular with the adolescent boys who were his students: "The fact that while dreaming of a girlfriend, we derive more pleasure from the dream than if we were really with her has no other cause than this: being that [during the dream] the external senses are constrained and dead (it is rightly said, in fact, that nature teaches us by dreaming to die) the imagination presents to the soul a more excellent image of the world."[35] The direct encounter with the girlfriend establishes a first principle, but she reaches human perfection not through her own nature but only through the muffling of the admirer's external senses by dreaming. Similarly, the application of logic to any experience makes it possible to make accurate judgments about the experience. That is what Cremonini meant by *paedia*. Cremonini was on the verge of making Descartes's move, and one can see why he was unwilling to see—that is, through the telescope. The senses cannot be trusted unless logic is also applied.

The practical disagreements between Cremonini and Galileo commenced after the appearance in fall 1604 of a supernova, the "new star" that intrigued Galileo, who had previ-

ously shown little interest in observational astronomy. He
made observations with the naked eye and compared his data
with those gathered in Verona and elsewhere, to reach the
conclusion that the supernova, when seen from different
places, did not demonstrate parallax, that is the apparent dis-
placement of an object relative to other objects due to the
observer's change of position. In a series of lectures in Padua
that drew huge audiences, Galileo explained how parallax
could be used to determine the location of objects on earth
or in the heavens and how the moon exhibited pronounced
parallax. Since the new star had no parallax, it had to be far
beyond the moon, probably among the fixed stars. His conclusion contradicted a fundamental principle of Aristotelian
physics whereby nothing new could be created beyond the
moon's orbit, which defined the outer limits within which re-
sided the natural elements that demonstrated conditions of
flux. The new star must be in a region where Aristotle had
said nothing could change.

Although Cremonini wrote nothing on the subject under
his own name, Galileo later remembered him as the most
troublesome adversary in the ensuing controversy. Stillman
Drake has convincingly argued that Cremonini was the author of a portion of the *Discourse on the New Star,* ostensi-
bly by Antonio Lorenzini of Montepulciano. Lorenzini described a debate at Padua between the philosophers and the
mathematicians, which was probably just between Cremonini
and Galileo rather than between the faculties of mathematics
and philosophy as a whole.[36] Galileo replied to *The Discourse*

in his own *Dialogue Concerning the New Star,* under the pseudonym Cecco di Ronchitti (Blindman of the Blind Alleys). The *Dialogue,* written in the Paduan dialect, was a debate between two Ruzante-like peasants who unmistakably referred to Cremonini in mentioning "a great Doctor of the Bo" and "men who are as thick as the great tower of Cremona," a reference to Cremonini's Falstaffian girth.[37] Cremonini echoed the criticisms of mathematics he had already presented in the *Tractatus de Paedia* and argued that it was bad physics to extrapolate from objects close at hand (and thus observable by the senses) to very distant objects. The apparent certainty of mathematics did not solve this problem. Cremonini argued for making appropriate inductions from experience, even if his understanding of experience derived from the Aristotelian theory of the elements and the unchangeability of the celestial sphere, which limited how distant the new star could be. His inductions demonstrated that something must be wrong with Galileo's mathematics. For his part, Galileo argued that if the question is how far away the star is, then all that matters is how one measures the distance. Every other consideration is irrelevant. As Drake pointed out, "Cremonini's position was in fact quite sound, though it lost out in the later science of the seventeenth century. The same may be said of Galileo's position. We are not dealing here with dunderheads, but only with losers."[38] Galileo's was a losing position simply because stars do exhibit parallax, a phenomenon that would not be observed, however, for another two hundred years.

The Inquisition judged Galileo the heretic, and history has judged Cremonini the loser. But Cremonini was certainly the more dangerous in his heresies. The nub of the matter, from the first disputes with the Jesuits to the Holy Office's postmortem denunciation of Cremonini's works, was his apparent denial of the immortality of the soul. Since virtually all students in the faculties of arts and medicine attended lectures in natural philosophy, the problem of the immortality of the soul was potentially more troublesome than any other subject taught at the university. The denial of the immortality of the soul implied at a minimum the rejection of the doctrine of Purgatory as a logical consequence, which aroused suspicions of Protestantism. However, his critics chose to interpret his rejection in the most damaging way, as a denial of the divine creation and the providence of God, because Cremonini also seemed to argue that the laws of physics and of the heavens operated independently of God.[39] By the 1590s these propositions had become dangerous territory, especially since the Church in the form of the Holy Office and the Society of Jesus had far more effective institutional structures for the enforcement of orthodoxy than it had had a century before.

The denial of the immortality of the soul signaled to orthodox thinkers rejection of the entire Christian message, and even the advocacy of atheism. Scholars have now firmly established that systematic, philosophically grounded atheism was "both conceivable and actual among the educated and the uneducated" in the sixteenth and seventeenth centuries, and especially in Italy.[40] Of course, the orthodox frequently hurled the charge of atheism at all sorts of nonconformists, and coming from inquisitors and orthodox theologians that charge must be taken with a grain of salt. Most of those who may have been atheists, such as Paolo Sarpi, recognized the dangers of openly avowing their unbelief and shared their views only with kindred thinkers who could be trusted. Giulio Cesare Vanini, however, publicly proclaimed his. Educated by Jesuits and himself a Carmelite monk, Vanini was in Padua in 1608 and preached in Venice a few years later. In a short book published in Paris in 1616, he systematically laid out the arguments against all the principal teachings of Christianity, including the argument for the existence of God. He was sentenced for atheism and burned to death in Toulouse in 1619.[41] Did Cremonini share the atheism of Vanini, whom he undoubtedly knew in Padua? The apparent rejection by Cremonini of the immortality of the soul brought him very close, but his public conformity to Catholic practice and open recommendation to others that they dissimulate makes it difficult to say how far in the direction of atheism his thinking went.

It might be more appropriate to ask whether Cremonini's apparent denial of the immortality of the soul was in fact another one of his masks. Was the denial, as some modern scholars have asserted, a pose he took as the professor teaching Aristotle at Padua—a self-imposed test, so to speak, of his logical and rhetorical skills—even though as a Christian he personally believed in immortality?[42] He was known as an expert on Alexander of Aphrodisias (born c. 200), whose most widely discussed work, *On the Soul,* had been intensely debated since the thirteenth century. These disputes were over the interpretation of Aristotle's views about personal immortality, and by discussing them Cremonini seemed to suggest that he accepted Alexander's view that the intellect does not survive the death of the physical body. Yet he treated the dangerous issue playfully. He was said to have written his own epitaph to read, *Hic jacet totius Cremoninus* ("Here lies all of Cremonini"), which may be an encapsulation of Alexander or a joke or both.[43] We have already seen how he refused to correct his own text to conform to orthodoxy and challenged the Holy Office to appoint someone else to do it for him, a challenge the prelates failed to accept. Among his friends he was notoriously slippery on the issue. In the *Dialogue Concerning the Two Chief World Systems* (1632), Galileo seems to be recounting a personal correspondence he had with Cremonini about the immortality of the soul:

> For it is not long since a famous philosopher composed a book on the soul in which, discussing Aristotle's opinion as to its mortality or immortality, he adduced many texts beyond those already quoted by Alexander. As to those, he asserted that Aristotle was not even dealing with such matters there, let alone deciding anything about them, and he gave others which he himself had discovered in various remote places and which tended to the damaging side. Being advised that this would make trouble for him in getting a license to publish it, he wrote back to his friend that he would never-

theless get one quickly, since if no other obstacle came up he
would have no difficulty altering the doctrine of Aristotle;
for with other texts and other expositions he could maintain
the contrary opinion, and it would still agree with the sense
of Aristotle.[44]

Cremonini's sophistry or the Nicodemite habit of maintaining a mental reservation while practicing public conformity
may be just another mask. His sense of playful intellectual
gamesmanship was what his students took to heart more
than any particular philosophical or theological position. In
fact, Cremonini's interpretation of Aristotle led to a dead
end, but his intellectual style had enormous influence on a
whole generation of thinkers in Padua, Venice, and beyond,
especially among those who came to be called the libertines.

His student Gabriel Naudé exported Cremonini's erudite
libertine views to France. Naudé noted Cremonini's favorite
maxim, "Intus ut libet, foris ut moris est" ("Think what you
like, but say what is expected of you," or "Inwardly according
to your will, outwardly according to social convention"), the
supreme expression of the libertine habit of living inside a
mask, of remaining "unknown," as the Accademia degli Incogniti, founded in Venice by Cremonini's students, proclaimed to be their goal.[45] According to Naudé's recollection,
Cremonini argued for a double truth, one theological and
one philosophical, a position that made him a powerful voice
for philosophical liberty. More than his skepticism, his alleged rejection of divine providence, or even his atheism, it
was his commitment to intellectual liberty that captured the

imagination of the libertines and made him their patron saint, if that is not an inappropriate term to use. Naudé is probably responsible for the reputation Italy gained as "full of libertines, atheists, and people who do not believe in anything." He discussed those who had written about the immortality of the soul, in an obvious reference to Cremonini, but suggested that one could not take their arguments at face value because their first principle is doubt. All their writings are fables about which no one can be certain of the meaning, because their purpose, rather than to instruct about positive truths, is to instill doubt about everything.[46]

The final doubt has to do with Cremonini's influence on literary theory. Just as the philosopher became the reactionary straw man in the Galilean debates about mathematics and scientific observation, he became the icon of retrograde poetic theory. Italian poets' creativity had long been inhibited by their stultifying imitation of Petrarchan language and grammar. In 1609 Alessandro Tassoni challenged the Petrarchan tradition and called for experimentation in new poetic forms. His irreverent attack had as its unnamed object none other than Cremonini, the exponent of retrograde poetic theory based on Aristotle's poetics. Padua became the epicenter of a debate about poetry and rhetoric in which "every battle for the affirmation of a literary theory became clouded by an Aristotelianism philologically equipped." The Paduan philosophical school, with Giuseppe degli Aromatari, coached by Cremonini, as its spokesman, united against Tassoni; but in the debates a certain carnivalesque playfulness took over, in which Cremonini's views were reversed, and the old conservative was cast as the innovator. In the heat of the debate the desire to preserve, and the will to defend, the unconditional liberty of thought collided in the land of Cockaigne, and since Cremonini managed to keep his own mask on and allowed Aromatari to face down Tassoni, it is still unclear where Cremonini stood.[47] One must assume, however, that he had strong views on poetics, for that is precisely one of the forms of literary activity that most intrigued his students.

What, then, was the cause of Cesare Cremonini's headache? Was it his reaction to Galileo's new discoveries? Was it his fear of the challenge the Jesuit fathers presented to his entrenched privileges? Was it the double life he led, as private skeptic and public believer masked by an Aristotelian commitment to a double truth? Was it a conflict between his rigid Aristotelianism and his desire for freedom of thought—that is, his libertine impulse? Was it the strain attendant on an intellectual game that transcended commitment to any principle? I do not really know, but I surmise that his friend Galileo did. Both these men who sometimes chose to be blind shared, I strongly suspect, a commitment to multiple forms of inquiry, which embraced Aristotelian logic, empirical research, and even theology, yet both refused to privilege any of these. Their students, especially Cremonini's, embraced the same commitment to freedom of thought and expression in their often outrageously skeptical and libertine works.

Thus, in late-Renaissance debates one can see the rudiments of culture wars that have sometimes turned intellectual life into a battlefield in our own times. On the one side was Christian orthodoxy promoted by the Jesuits, who advocated a universal educational program open to all—whether rich man or poor man, nobleman or commoner—by emphasizing basic skills over intellectual flexibility, inculcating fundamental truths rather than encouraging creative exploration, and promoting ethical behavior rather than personal indulgence. On the other side were thinkers who did not necessarily agree on fundamental truths, other than their commitment to open-ended methods of inquiry that left room for revision, modification, and debate; to a pedagogy that treated the teacher-student relationship as reciprocal; and to a life of personal fulfillment. Then as now, the bastion of the first approach was the Church, and the bastion of the second the university; and the objective of both was to conquer the minds of youth.

TWO

The Libertines

THE CELESTIAL
DIVORCE

I n 1642 Maffeo Barberini (aka Pope Urban VIII) provoked the War of Castro against the Farnese duke of Parma. During this grubby little war, scandalous for the opportunism of the Barberini, even by the scandalous standards of the seventeenth century, one of the most popular and controversial authors of the day, Ferrante Pallavicino, completed the first volume of a proposed trilogy, *The Celestial Divorce (Il Divortio celeste)*. A biting satirist and unrelenting critic of the Barberini papacy, Pallavicino was already more an enemy of Pope Urban than Galileo had been (he had died the previous January, still under house arrest). *The Celestial Divorce* depicted Jesus Christ seeking out the Eternal Father to announce his wish to divorce his bride, the Roman Church, who had committed intolerable adulteries and lived in a cesspool of vice. In order to inform himself about the state of things, God the Father, presumably because he could not trust St. Peter, sent St. Paul down to earth to visit Rome. Paul returned so scandalized that he recommended that the Father grant Christ's request. The first volume ended at this point, but the other volumes, if they had been completed, were to continue with an account of how Luther, Calvin, and Mark of Ephesus (the fifteenth-century Greek theologian who had opposed the unification of the Greek and Roman churches) offered their own churches as the new bride of Christ. After considering their suitability for matrimony, Christ was to have demurred, stating that he did not intend to wed any of the existing churches.[1]

By the time Pallavicino satirized the Roman Church in *The Celestial Divorce*, the Venice-centered culture wars of the late Renaissance, which had begun in the 1590s with the conflict between the Society of Jesus and the faculty of the University of Padua, had become thoroughly embedded in actual wars, not just the local War of Castro but the much more violent conflict between the Habsburgs and the Bourbons, between Catholic and Protestant powers, now known as the Thirty Years' War. The culture wars had already turned nasty in Venice. An ardent defender of the liberty of the Venetian republic, Galileo's old friend Paolo Sarpi, had been stabbed and gravely wounded on a Venetian bridge in 1607, allegedly by papal agents. Even after the end of the papal interdict against Venice, the Society of Jesus remained banished from the Venetian republic, which until the 1650s was the font of

I L
DIVORTIO
CELESTE,

CAGIONATO DALLE
dissolutezze della Sposa
Romana ,

E T

Consacrato alla simplicità
de'Scropolosi Chri-
stiani.

In Ingolstatt. 1643.

Per Iosef Arlstozz.

Title page to Ferrante Pallavicino, *Il Divortio celeste*
(Ingolstadt, 1643).

antipapal, and some would say atheistic, thought in Italy. As long as authors did not attack the government of Venice itself, they could publish almost anything in Venice, and they did. The papal nuncio and the Roman inquisitors maintained an extensive network of spies in the city and filled the archives in Rome with correspondence about the antipapal press in Venice, but the Venetian Senate, despite serious internal divisions on religious issues, usually protected controversial authors. A whole new literary economy arose during the seventeenth century, which evolved most fully in Venice but also connected the lagoon city with international intellectual and political developments. The new literary economy produced a tremendous variety of printed works, including broadsheets—the prototype for modern newspapers—pamphlets that popularized many new trends, *novellas*, poems, and opera libretti. One Venetian printer, Girolamo Albrizzi, turned out many different kinds of books—tourists' yearbooks, almanacs, and broadsheets—that is, he printed anything that could bring him a profit. Within this new literary economy, religious skepticism and libertine views found a ready market.[2] Despite Venice's reputation as a safe haven, the international situation exacerbated cultural and religious tensions, especially after the beginning of the Thirty Years' War, and many authors besides Pallavicino resorted to pseudonyms, anonymity, and publication in Protestant countries.

Ferrante Pallavicino, born in Parma in 1615, was among the youngest of the prolific authors who dominated the Venetian scene during the 1630s and '40s. In Milan he took the white habit of the Lateranensi canons, from whom he received the typical training for religious novices in a curriculum heavily influenced by the Jesuit model. While still a teenager he obtained leave from his superior to visit the Lateranensi in France, but instead of going abroad, he left for Venice, where he found a girlfriend, lived incognito, and wrote exuberant letters back to his superior and fellow canons describing the trip to France he never took. He then went to Padua, where he apparently enrolled in some courses at the university. The University of Padua was still in the thrall of the philosophical skepticism of Cesare Cremonini, who had died in 1631. While there, Pallavicino published his first book, *Il Sole ne' pianeti, cioè le grandezze della Serenissima Republica di Venetia* (The Sun in the planets, that is, the greatness of the Most Serene Republic of Venice), a panegyric that brought him the protection of the Venetian Senate.[3] In 1635 he returned to Venice for reasons of love, according to a contemporary biographer; he found there a hospitable environment for attacking what he imagined were his personal adversaries: the Society of Jesus, the Spanish monarchy, and the court of Rome. Despite his lively intellectual rebellion against the three pillars of Catholic orthodoxy, he did not renounce his vows but continued to live in Venice at the Lateranensi monastery of the Carità, now the museum of the Accademia di Belle Arti. At the monastery he spent two or three hours every morning writing in bed. He published his first drafts without correction, and in less than eight highly productive years he had produced twenty-six books and *novellas*. His evenings he spent frolicking with prostitutes, for whom he developed a powerful fascination that revealed a deep ambivalence about sexuality, also displayed in many of his writings.

His profligate ways made it necessary to have a patron, and he found one in the person of Giovanni Francesco Loredan (1607–1661), a member of one of Venice's most prominent patrician families and the founder of the famous Accademia degli Incogniti. For a time Pallavicino served as Loredan's private secretary, and over the years Loredan, who was eight years older than Pallavicino, provided for his financial and publishing needs. Loredan worked his way up the cursus honorum of Venetian offices; by the 1650s he had held such influential posts as state inquisitor and membership in the Council of Ten and the Minor Council, offices that placed him within the inner circle of Venetian politicians. Through his political influence Loredan protected the fashionable Incogniti, meanwhile using the academy and his own literary works, such as his *novella Diana* (Venice, 1635), to further his anti-Habsburg program. The interpretive key to *Diana* was an anagram composed of the names of the protagonists of the Thirty Years' War, including Wallenstein, Gustavus Adolphus, and Maria Habsburg, who was cast as Diana herself. Along with a number of other Incognito publications that touched upon the Thirty Years' War, *Diana* was republished numerous times in the fifty years following the first edition. The book, in presenting Gustavus Adolphus as the hero of the war, marks the first time any Italian writer had openly praised a Protestant prince. Even Sarpi had never spoken favorably in public about a Protestant, but it was typical of the Incogniti to challenge the accepted norms by redefining the issue. What attracted them to the great Swede was not his Protestantism but his "natural" virtue.[4]

The Accademia degli Incogniti was active from about 1630 to 1660. Its members included nearly every important Venetian intellectual of the mid-seventeenth century and many prominent foreigners. In fact, foreign members outnumbered Venetians, a measure of the academy's international character. At the heart of Venetian cultural life, the Incogniti and the other fashionable academies created an intellectual style that depended on "conversation." The most important conversational activity was the oral presentation followed by debate. They created an "academic" style that placed enormous emphasis on the virtuosity of word selection and the power of language, not just for self-expression, but as an instrument for perception and deeper cognition. This was a trait borrowed from the Socratic methods of Cremonini, with whom so many of the Incogniti had studied. Their word play, their sense of the indeterminacy of meaning, and their understanding of language as a dynamic process rather than a fixed text betray a sensibility akin to that found in Montaigne's *Essays*. Loredan's *Spirit of Ferrante Pallavicino* borrowed from Montaigne the phrase *se promener* to explain the work of the Incogniti, as always in transition, a body of work in which meaning slid past any straightforward denotation. Other such borrowings from French included *rapsodie, fricassée, pot-pourri, mosaique*.[5]

The Incogniti transformed their private academic debates involving speaking and listening into the more public forms of theatrical production and publishing. Musical theater was one of their favored genres. The Incogniti supported the most successful opera theater of the 1640s, the Novissimo. Besides writing opera libretti, they published moral and religious tracts, philosophical essays, and especially *novellas* that have come to be labeled libertine.[6] Their wide-ranging and eclectic works betrayed certain preoccupations, including an interest in kabbalistic magic, eroticism tinged with overt homosexuality, parodies of the Christian virtues, blasphemy, and religious speculations that were certainly heterodox and skeptical.

The Incogniti often hid their ideas and identities behind metaphorical language and pseudonyms. Loredan, for example, used the comical anglicized pseudonym Henrico Giblet. The overt justification for their secrecy was the poetic commonplace that the truth must remain hidden from the prying eyes of the vulgar, and their explicit models were Cremonini, who advocated a calculated dissimulation, and Montaigne, who had placed the truth "at the back of the shop" (*à l'arrière-boutique*). The motto of the Incogniti was *Ex ignoto notus* ("The known from the unknown"), which appeared in their books on an emblem that depicted the Nile, an allusion to the river's unknown origins.[7] Despite their propensity for playful secrets, they displayed a converse and apparently irresistible fascination for publicity, exemplified by Girolamo Brusoni's 1647 panegyric of the Incogniti. *The*

Glories of the Incogniti supplied pocket biographies and a list of the publications of 104 members, who came from all over Italy and as far away as Copenhagen and the Greek island of Chios. According to the incomplete list in *The Glories,* the membership of the Incogniti included more Bolognese (thirteen) than Venetians (eleven), and significant contingents of Genoese (nine) and Milanese (six). The Accademia degli Incogniti was hardly an exclusively Venetian institution; rather, it was a cosmopolitan Italian academy that took advantage of the relatively free political and intellectual environment of the Venetian republic; what unified most of the membership was not Venetian citizenship but the shared experience of study at Padua.[8]

Cesare Cremonini exercised the most powerful influence on the Incogniti. In his forty-year teaching career he was said to have had more students than any other professor at the university. In 1600 both Cremonini and Galileo were elected to the Accademia dei Ricoverati, upon which the Incogniti were partially modeled. Despite the fact that he defended the Aristotelian dictum that philosophy must be founded on sensory experiences, Cremonini embedded himself in a bookish rather than an experimental culture, and that tendency persisted among his students, few of whom seem to have been engaged in Galileo's new science.[9]

Cremonini's theory of the mortality of the soul bound up bodily sensations with the operations of the soul, which meant that sexual and other physical drives should be not suppressed but expressed. Skeptical of the Christian doc-

Ex ignoto notus ("The known from the unknown"), motto and emblem of the Incogniti. The engraving depicts the Nile River flowing from its then unknown source to its well-known delta. From Girolamo Brusoni, Jacopo Gaddi, or Giovanni Francesco Loredan (?), *Le Glorie degl'Incogniti* (Venice, 1647), facing page 1.

trines of salvation, Cremonini preached the value of physical pleasure over conventional Christian morality, a message that certainly struck a chord with the young students.[10] Cremonini's teachings about the mortality of the soul and his naturalistic philosophy constituted the grounding for the subversion of Christian moral values, especially sexual ethics.[11]

Having sat at the feet of Cremonini, the Incogniti kept alive in their academy his playful intellectual sensibility if not his rigid Aristotelianism. They loved to debate issues from as many points of view as they could imagine, creating an atmosphere in which witty, provocative conversation was valued, but which was morally equivocal or ambivalent. Typical of their work was Loredan's *Academic Novelties* (*Bizzarrie academiche*, 1654), which included discourses on whether blushing was a sign of virtue or vice, whether morality applied to card games, why old people sleep less than young people, why physicians have long beards, what the perils of sacrilegious love were, and why Pythagorus prohibited the use of fava beans. Many of Loredan's discourses are obscene commentaries, all dressed up with learned citations, on the effects of sexual desire on lovers.[12]

One of the mottos of the academy referred to the *Ignoto Deo*, the unknown God, an allusion to the academicians' fondness for preserving anonymity, operating behind the scenes, and writing in a secret code. The frontispiece of Loredan's *novella Amorous Doubts* (*Dubbi amorosi*) shows the author kneeling reverently before a figure that is entirely veiled and labeled *Ignoto Deo*. As Bernard Aikema has demonstrated, the engraving is overtly blasphemous. The phrase "the unknown god" alluded to St. Paul's sermon informing the Athenians that the inscription "To an unknown god" in one of their temples actually referred to the Christian God of the creation (Acts 17:23). The Loredan frontispiece, however, introduces a book about erotic love, and a cupid figure presents the author to his beloved, whom Loredan worships as if she were God.[13] Thus, a well-known passage of Scripture was deployed as the image of an idolatrous sexual obsession.

Gino Benzoni, the most prominent scholar of seventeenth-century Venetian intellectual life, evokes the sensibility of the seventeenth-century academicians, who with "the excitations of the pen" produced "waves of ink" in their effort to become authors.

> But authors of what? Above all of myriad little dissertations, through which passed into print the exploding sparkle of the changeable effervescences and fancies of academic conversation produced as "capricci" of the occasion, of spontaneous "abortions," of "jokes" more or less "genial," of "oddities" more or less eccentric, of gossipy "lapses." These were a pretext for the argument in favor of an affected improvisation in which futility is feigned, while the argument is serious and grave, even if in fact the consequence is really futile. Garrulous cicadas gathered in the academies. There they recited, with great precision, their blatherings. And then they published them.[14]

These publications contained frequent whiffs of heterodoxy. Loredan wrote essays on "nothing," and, in fact, the In-

This engraving of the Glories of the Incogniti depicts an obscure allegory, typical of the Incogniti, who sought to hide their meanings. Hercules, complete with club and lion's skin, sits pensively. Beneath his left arm is the emblem of the Incogniti, showing the Nile River flowing from its source to its delta, an illustration of the motto "The known from the unknown." Above Hercules the goddess Diana is about to spear a winged demon that perhaps with ironic intent bears a banner inscribed with the title of the book. Initial engraving in Girolamo Brusoni, Jacopo Gaddi, or Giovanni Francesco Loredan (?), *Le Glorie degl' Incogniti* (Venice, 1647).

cogniti had a certain fascination with nothing that permitted them to present "arguments from nothing" and "concepts of nothing." As Benzoni put it, "one can say that about nothing one is saying nothing. And he who does not say anything is not culpable of anything."[15] Although many of the Incogniti discourses on nothingness now seem quite silly, Benzoni's dismissal of them misses what was innovative and powerful in them. Rooted in the Greek Sophists' discussions about nothingness, the Renaissance debate about the "paradoxes on nothing" reappeared among several Incogniti writers in the 1630s.[16] For the Incognito Luigi Manzini, author of *Nothing* (*Il Niente*, 1634), celebrating the nobility of nothingness opened a door onto aesthetic and semiotic theory. Examining nothingness was a device for exploring the impossibility of representation in language, which led to a distrust of verbal language and to the cultivation of stylistic extremes for their shock value or, to put it in seventeenth-century terms, for the capacity of poetry to achieve novelty and produce the marvelous. One of the most influential poets in the history of Italian literature, Giovanbattista Marino (1569–1625), was a favorite of the Incogniti and the subject of a biography by Loredan. Marino is known as the author of the motto "The aim of the poet is to marvel," an objective that especially influenced the Incogniti authors.[17]

Any simple label that attempts to define these "excitations of the pen" does not do full justice to their diversity and rhetorical playfulness. The enemies of the Incogniti coined the most common label, "libertine," but one recent critic would prefer the description "proto-Enlightenment," and, as I hope to show, there is much to recommend this view.[18] The French Jesuit Father Garasse wrote a diatribe, *The Curious Doctrine of the Free Spirits* (1623), in which he defined the libertine as someone who identified God with nature, who denied transcendence, the reality of miracles, the immortality of the soul, and the otherworldly destiny of mankind. The libertine replaced free will and individual moral responsibility with a naturalistic determinism. The libertine considered all religious as political opportunists, and priests as impostors. The libertine embraced an instinctual ethic. As Father Garasse wrote, "there are a few free spirits in the world, and . . . they are not capable of believing in our doctrine. They do not speak openly but in secret and among other free spirits, confidants, and cabalists." He proposed a central proposition from which their doctrines derived: "The libertines are free spirits, strange persons, who attempt to enter into the secret of natural causes."[19] That definition would make even Galileo a libertine.

The libertinism of the Incogniti could get out of bounds. Through Loredan's personal intervention, the *novella The Schoolboy Alcibiades (Alcibiade fanciullo a scuola)* was published in Venice in 1650. This tale of pederastic seduction has been attributed to the Incognito Antonio Rocco—a student of theology and philosophy at the Collegio Romano and later of Cremonini at Padua. A Benedictine, he eventually taught philosophy in the convent attached to Andrea Palladio's magnificent San Giorgio Maggiore in Venice and turned down offers of university chairs at Padua and Pisa in order to stay in Venice as the public lecturer in moral philosophy. He refused to say Mass and was reputed to be an atheist.[20] The book centers on a dialogue between the Greek tutor Filotomo and his pupil Alcibiades in which the older man convinces his young pupil to yield to his sexual advances. An underground book during the seventeenth century, *Alcibiade* certainly had readers, and it directly influenced both Pietro della Vecchia's painting *Socrates and His Two Pupils* (also called *Know Thyself*) and the libretto for the Venetian opera *Alcibiade* (1680) by Aurelio Aureli. The preface to the libretto echoes the *novella* in its defense of the subject matter: "You will enjoy a few lascivious though restrained actions, composed by me with the sole aim that you learn to shun them, and not to imitate them." Sure. Rocco had defended himself through a surfeit of paradoxes. In "On Ugliness" he equates the ugly with hell and the beautiful with heaven and then reverses them, making hell the desired place and heaven the worse place. Loredan calls this display of moral gymnastics "most excellent," but it reads like sophistry now.[21]

Rocco's inquisition file is even more revealing than his published sophistries. Among the several denunciations of him is one filed in 1648 by Enrico Palladio, a physician from Udine, who fell deathly ill. To clear his conscience, he called to his bed the inquisitors of Udine, to report conversations he had had in Venice with Rocco. For about two and a half years, Palladio had tagged along with some friends who went to play cards in Rocco's lodgings at San Moisè.

Every time I wanted to, I could go into the bedroom of Signor Rocco, where he was always ill, and talk with him. He spoke languidly because of the infirmity of his soul and said, "Oh, my soul, I know that you have to go and I know where you will go; it will be over soon." Moreover, many times he offered me his book *On the Mortality of the Soul (De mortalitate animae)*, and he wanted to make me give it to his students, but I neglected to look at it, and once he asked if I had read it, and I told him yes, even though I had not read it. . . .

Likewise the said Signor Rocco once told me that one finds in the Holy Scriptures many contradictions and things that do not coincide with the proper time period, and things that cannot be so, in particular the Ark of Noah, which could not be capable of carrying so many animals. . . .

Also Signor Rocco asked us how much time since we had been used carnally, either naturally or against nature, and we told him all about it; and he added, "You have done well because that instrument was made by nature because we have our tastes and delights."[22]

What interested the inquisitors, however, was less Rocco's sodomies than his heresies, especially his rejection of the immortality of the soul after the fashion of Cremonini.

For all their free-spirited ideas, the Incogniti were hardly revolutionaries. No matter how much they rebelled against the dogmas of the Church, they failed to imagine an alternative society or to embrace an ideology of progress, as would the Enlightenment thinkers whom the Incogniti anticipated in other respects. In fact, they remained, as Giorgio Spini put it, "fixed in a fundamentally conservative attitude," insensible

Pietro della Vecchia's painting *Socrates and His Two Pupils*, also known as *Know Thyself*, was one of a series of oil paintings Vecchia produced showing an elderly teacher paying what may be seen as erotic attention to his young students. Antonio Rocco's book advocating pedophilia influenced della Vecchia. Prado Museum, Madrid.

to the sources for social renewal in their own time. Spini traced the attitude of the Venetian libertines to the influence of Cremonini, who had oriented them toward a backward-looking philosophical and historical method and who seems to have imparted to a chosen few intimates the rudiments of his crypto-libertinism.[23] Thus, in politics they uncritically promulgated the conservative, traditional myth about the virtues of the Venetian republic.

Loredan himself depicted the academies as a microcosm of that republic. In his *Academic Novelties,* he presented a discourse on "that thing which is most prejudicial to the survival of the academies." He defines the academy as "none other than a union of the Virtuous to cheat time, and to investigate Virtue and happiness." Quoting Plato, Loredan defines the republic in the same way, as a union of citizens for the purpose of pursuing happiness. The first obligation of academicians is to flee error, and of the citizen to avoid blame. The function of the academy is to teach, and the interests of the academy and the republic are virtually identical. He then examines those things prejudicial to both republics and academies. His list is a peculiar amalgam of republican theory with a certain Incognito twist. The prejudicial conditions he catalogs include: when rewards and punishments are determined by emotions rather than justice, when merit is not rewarded, when citizens are unequal, and when those who govern are ignorant. This is standard republican theory. But he slips in between numbers three and five—the position rhetorical theory designated as the least conspicuous on his list—the statement "Old age is a grave detriment to the interests of the Republic."[24] Is this an example of the Incogniti's questioning the gerontocracy of *savi* who governed them, without bringing the republican system itself into question?[25]

The Incogniti supported the most ardent of the free spirits, Ferrante Pallavicino, and provided an appreciative audience for him. The books he wrote during his most productive period, between 1635 and 1640, were so popular that booksellers and printers bought them from him at a premium. During the same half decade, he worked on publishing projects with the Incogniti and another prominent academy, the Unisoni. He also published accounts of his travels to Genoa and to Germany as the chaplain to the duke of Amalfi. After the German trip he returned to Venice in the summer of 1541 with his face disfigured by a skin disease and a new book ready for publication. *Il Corriero svaligiato*, which might be translated as "The Post-Boy Robbed of His Bag," became, according to his contemporary biographer and colleague in the Incogniti, Girolamo Brusoni, the "sole cause of all his misfortunes."[26] In the *novella* four courtiers read and comment on letters that their prince has ordered stolen from a courier. The letters included some political ones written by the Spanish governor of Milan. The conceit of the *novella* allowed Pallavicino to express multiple points of view and to offer a small encyclopedia of contemporary ideologies critical of the "Grandi," described as ravenous wolves and greedy harpies; the court of Urban VIII Barberini, "the barber who cut the beard of Christ"; the Jesuits who attempted to mo-

This frontispiece engraving is typical of the Venetian tradition of female personifications of the Republic of Venice, presiding over the sea empire symbolized by the ship on the left and the land empire depicted as a tower on a hill. From Giovanni Francesco Loredan, *Discorsi academici de' Signori incogniti* (Venice, 1635).

nopolize all education and intellectual life; the Inquisition, which ruined the business of publishers through prosecution of those who sold prohibited books; and most of all of the Spanish, who dominated Italy politically and militarily. The only powers to escape condemnation in the letters were the valiant republics, Genoa, Lucca, and especially Venice, which had managed to maintain political independence.[27]

The reaction against *Il Corriero svaligiato* was immediate. The apostolic nuncio to Venice, Francesco Vitelli, demanded Pallavicino's arrest; Pallavicino spent six months in Venetian prisons but was never brought to trial.[28] In March 1642 the supporters of the Holy See in the Senate proposed legislation to banish Pallavicino and prohibit the sale of *Il Corriero.* The proposal came to a vote four times and failed to pass, for each time more senators abstained than voted for the provision. With the support of Loredan and the Incogniti, Pallavicino mustered strong backing from many members of the upper levels of the Venetian patriciate, even if most were unwilling to commit themselves to a "no" vote.[29] Nevertheless, after his release from prison he lived insecurely in Venice, tenaciously persecuted by Vitelli and the nephew of the pope, Francesco Barberini. Twice Pallavicino was forced to leave his monastery and take refuge with Loredan, and during the summer of 1642 he escaped Venice, traveling home to Parma, to Friuli, and back to Parma, only to return to Venice in August to see a woman.

Even while he was in prison and later on the run from the nuncio, Pallavicino had not backed off from his attacks on the pope. He published clandestinely and anonymously, but the sellers of his books were severely punished, and a professional spy identified Pallavicino to the nuncio as the offending author. During the eighteen months after the publication of *Il Corriero svaligiato* he wrote four books, including a trilogy of anti-Barberini works that blamed Pope Urban for the War of Castro and for machinations aimed at achieving domination of Italy (the *Baccinata, Dialogo molto curioso,* and *Il Divortio celeste*), and the scandalous anti-Jesuit work *The Rhetoric of Whores (La Retorica delle puttane),* which was "dedicated to the guild of the most celebrated courtesans."[30]

More than any of his other books, *The Rhetoric of Whores* demonstrates why Pallavicino was the only Italian author of his epoch capable of a coherent vision that integrated satire, skepticism, and naturalistic morality.[31] The book is a didactic lecture on the relation between rhetoric and philosophy, in which an old prostitute instructs a naive apprentice. The old woman is in bad health, poor, and miserable, all because she "did not know to stop at rhetoric, wanting to go on to learn philosophy"; in other words, she did not understand that her profession relies on deception, and she made the mistake of falling in love. By "rhetoric," she means the arts of simulation and dissimulation, which would have brought her pleasure and riches, without danger, while philosophy, with its pretension to discovering truth, has brought her the ruin of emotional authenticity. In many respects, however, the book is a paradox: on the one hand a manual on the arts of deception shared by prostitutes and rhetoricians, and on the other

Portrait of Ferrante Pallavicino from an engraving in Girolamo
Brusoni, Jacopo Gaddi, or Giovanni Francesco Loredan (?), *Le
Glorie degl' Incogniti* (Venice, 1647), p. 136.

an unmasking of rhetoric, a warning about its "artificial words and mendacious pretexts," which require vigilance. Nevertheless, when it comes to exploring the arts of "carnal pleasure," Pallavicino drops his ironic tone and straightforwardly declares that sexual satisfaction is completely legitimate and natural, on a level with urinating.[32] In the "Author's Confession" at the end, Pallavicino reverts to the Aristotelian philosophy of his generation's mentor, Cesare Cremonini, stating that all sexual desire is "natural," not because reproduction is natural but because retention of semen leads to death by poisoning. Thus, the implications of Cremonini's naturalistic philosophy are pushed to their most extreme ends, ones echoed in Rocco's defense of pederasty. But Pallavicino entered what may have been even more dangerous shoals than Rocco.

Pallavicino put into the mouth of the old whore lessons paraphrased from Cipriano Suarez's *De arte rhetorica*, the manual read in the Jesuit schools. In fifteen lessons for young future prostitutes, *The Rhetoric of Whores* is structured according to the subdivisions of Suarez's textbook for young future Jesuits. Although Pallavicino claims in his introduction to be writing a morality tale about the false lures of commercial sex, he fooled no one, least of all the Inquisitors of the Holy Office. It is obvious that the "artificial lies," "deceptions" *(inganni)*, and "wickednesses" *(ribalderie)* of the courtesan were also the principal ingredients in a Jesuit education. The old whore was teaching the beautiful young girl the trade by taking the teachings of the Society of Jesus as a model for the arts of seduction. Pallavicino's work had precedents—especially in the connection Aretino drew between rhetorical expertise and erotic perversion—but *The Rhetoric of Whores* is a "strange achievement" without precedent. In the words of James Grantham Turner, "All satirical applications of the 'University' curriculum to advanced sexual practice generate a shadowy endorsement of the conceit they intend to render unthinkable—the idea of bringing sexuality from the mute realm of 'Nature' into the domain of discursive construction, under female supervision."[33] By systematically pursuing the parallels between rhetorical persuasion and erotic seduction, Pallavicino demonstrates how the high art of rhetoric has the same instrumental character as the lowly deceptions of the prostitute. In the end Pallavicino's offensive against the Society of Jesus, the Spanish ambassadors in Italy, and the Barberini pope meant that even Venice was no longer a safe haven for him. In the autumn of 1642, Pallavicino escaped to Bergamo, where he completed the first volume of *The Celestial Divorce*, which came to be known, in the words of a contemporary, as "superior to all others in impiety and blasphemies against the Roman Church."[34] In Bergamo Pallavicino was awaiting the arrival of an acquaintance, Charles de Brèche, a French knight known in Italy under the pseudonym Carlo di Morfì, who had recently befriended Pallavicino while the two were traveling on a *traghetto* from Padua to Venice and had "accidentally" bumped into him numerous times in book shops in Venice. The affable and flattering Morfì told the ambitious young author that none other than Cardinal

LA
RETORICA

DELLE

PVTTANE

*Compoſta conforme li precetti
di Cipriano.*

DEDICATA

Alla vniuerſità delle Cortegiane più
Celebri.

In Cambrai, 1642.

Con licenza de' Superiori, e priuilegio.

Title page of Ferrante Pallavicino, *La Retorica delle
puttane* (Cambrai, 1642).

Richelieu greatly admired his books and showed Pallavicino forged letters and commissions offering him a large stipend as the cardinal's official historian if he were to come to France. Pallavicino took the bait, and after Morfí arrived in Bergamo, the two set off for Paris around the middle of November, Pallavicino traveling under the false name of Raimondi. Cardinal Richelieu died on December 4, but Morfí somehow convinced Pallavicino to continue along a route that was not, in fact, leading toward Paris. As the two rode their horses across one of the famous bridges of Avignon, celebrated in verse and song, Pallavicino spotted the papal insignia and sensed a trap. He turned his horse to flee but was soon overtaken by a squad of beadles who had been put on alert. In Pallavicino's black leather bag, the police discovered a number of compromising manuscripts and threw him into the dreaded Tower of the Latrines.

The home of the papacy between 1309 and 1377, Avignon had been an Apostolic legation since 1433, which made it a part of the Papal States. The cardinal legate had sovereign powers over the territory, including supreme judicial authority in civil, criminal, and canon law cases. At the moment Pallavicino was arrested, the cardinal legate was the pope's nephew, Antonio Barberini, and the vice legate was a candidate for a red hat and client of the Barberini, Federico Sforza. Pallavicino had fallen into the hands of his most determined enemies. He continued to insist that he was really named Raimondi, but since he had published his most controversial books under pseudonyms and some were in his possession, it did not really matter what his name was. Early in 1643, while he was still imprisoned, *The Celestial Divorce* was published, based on a manuscript Pallavicino had turned over to a press in Geneva on his way to France. The book was an immediate sensation, and not only in Italy, where bookshops sold it under the counter. It was plagiarized in Protestant countries, and soon editions appeared in German, Swedish, French, Dutch, and English.

Proceedings against him did not begin until the following August. On the basis of evidence transmitted by the papal legate in Venice, Pallavicino was forced to admit his true identity and acknowledge his authorship of several recent anonymous books satirizing the Barberini and the Jesuits. A sentence of death for lèse majesté was a foregone conclusion. On March 5, 1644, the twenty-eight-year-old Pallavicino was executed in Avignon by decapitation. Five months later the flagrant nepotist Urban VIII was himself dead. By the end of 1646, Charles de Brèche, Pallavicino's false friend Morfí, died by an assassin's knife, whether or not in revenge for Pallavicino's death is unknown.

Pallavicino's death, needless to say, dealt a heavy blow to his colleagues in the Accademia degli Incogniti. The shock silenced the usually garrulous group. When they returned to speaking and writing, they masked their true meaning in even more obscure linguistic codes and clouds of metaphor and became very cautious about saying or writing anything that might be hateful to the ears of the powerful. Loredan's comments about the "martyr of truth" are revealing. He concluded that it is "imprudent to write and comment on the actions of living princes." He recommended that those who wrote about princes should only praise them—should exercise "prudence of the pen." The Incogniti had felt the bitter consequences of their claim that truth and satire were one and the same. And they began to distance themselves from Pallavicino's legacy, referring to him as an "unquiet spirit with a fleeting mind and confused thoughts." He had not understood that it was "a crime to speak the truth."[35]

Besides the arbiters of Catholic orthodoxy, one of Pallavicino's most common targets was women. Pallavicino's misogyny was hardly without parallel, but as was also true of his attacks on the Barberini papacy, it had an especially vitriolic character. What makes his misanthropy worth paying attention to today is the rhetorical drubbing he received from Suor Arcangela Tarabotti. The fifth letter in Pallavicino's *Il Corriero svaligiato* is addressed to an "Ungrateful Woman" and is an essay on the tropes of misogyny.

> If you are looking for sphinxes, panthers, tigers, and other wild beasts or monsters, *cherchez la femme!* A single woman, and you will find all the most savage animals and brutish natures together in one entity. As a rule, one does not find in your sex any rational capacity other than the will, so submerged by the passions that it has become an irrefutable axiom to say that woman is without judgment. Whether her lust is boundless or her rages out of control, she knows no moderation, a quality from which one is led to draw the conclusion that a person is human. So when she would have us

believe that she has plundered some human traits—gentle appearances, tender charms, and courteous behavior—let it also be said that she has stolen seduction from the siren, cunning tricks from another monster, and that she dresses in disguise to accomplish treachery. Like an octopus camouflaged on the reef to capture its prey, she transforms herself with a show of male qualities to facilitate her lies.[36]

Tarabotti defended women through her counterassault on men: "Oh, you wicked hypocrites, you devils incarnate, not unlike your master in your feigned expressions, your calculated betrayals, your false promises and all the rest, as only you know better! Not for nothing is the word 'demon' (*demone*) of the masculine gender, as if the female sex does not deserve to have attributed to it any of the names of Hell's infernal monsters."[37] Tarabotti could not resist turning Pallavicino's own misfortunes against him.

And there is also another modern author, whose name I shall pass over in silence. He too invents shameful insults against our sex with his satirical viper's tongue in a loathsome work. What a liar, and malicious to boot, especially in letter 5— just as well he was put to death before the book's publication! Little wonder if he defaces woman's sacred features; he is guilty of sacrilege against the entire Catholic Church. He respects neither pope nor cardinals nor the Roman Curia; and he uses strident vituperation to lash out against all Christendom.[38]

She systematically dismantled the arguments in letter 5, down to the point of turning Pallavicino's metaphors upside down to work for the benefit of women rather than to their detriment. "This detractor has also blabbered on about woman being like the vine, forgetting that the simile may also be turned to woman's advantage: from the vine, after all, nourishment of human life is pressed, that precious liquid that increases our bodily heat and therefore our vital fluids and life itself."[39]

Tarabotti was herself among the most celebrated and controversial authors of her day with her books on *Convent Life as Paradise* (1643), *Against Female Luxury, Menippean Satire, Antisatire* (1644), *Familiar Letters* (1650), *Women Are No Less Rational Than Men* (1651), *Paternal Tyranny*, which was retitled *Innocence Betrayed* before publication (1654), and the scandalous tract that was widely circulated in manuscript but unpublished in her lifetime, *Convent Life as Hell*. Perhaps what is most intriguing is that Tarabotti relied on the same patronage network as Pallavicino, the Accademia degli Incogniti, and especially its founder Giovanni Francesco Loredan. She was the only woman writer to have earned Loredan's support, which may have come through the intervention of her brother-in-law, Giacomo Pighetti, who was himself a member. Her relationship with the Incogniti, however, was even more complicated than the paradox inherent in the reliance of a Benedictine nun on the notoriously anti-Catholic and libertine academy might suggest. The complexity of the relationship is an indicator of how intellectually open-minded the Incogniti really were. A letter from Loredan praising Tarabotti's "trees of learning" introduces her *Convent Life as Paradise,* and she dedicated her own published correspondence to him. He acted as her editor, helped get her books published, and introduced her to his circle of friends and visiting intellectuals. He published some of his letters to her and dedicated to her part of his *novella Abraham*. But they also could be highly critical of each other. Her *Antisatire* was a response to a satire delivered before the Incogniti, and Loredan took her critique as a personal affront and accused her of ingratitude. Another Incognito wrote a sustained attack on her and even accused her of being incapable of having written a book as fine as *Convent Life as Paradise*. After her own brother-in-law criticized her work, she responded caustically that "knowing very well that virtue is broken and bungled in women," she would no longer seek male approval. And yet the *Antisatire* was put out by the press known as the publisher for the Incogniti. The publisher stated that he had stolen the manuscript from Tarabotti, who did not want her polemic in print, a claim we should take with a grain of salt. Her *Paternal Tyranny* takes on not just Pallavicino's misogynous letter but Loredan's *novella The Life of Adam*.[40] It is obvious that nothing about the Incogniti was straightforward and there was always more to their doings than meets the eye. Perhaps it is best to think about the academy, its debates, and its relations with the lame nun with the acerbic pen as a kind of theater. It is not always clear whether someone is playing a role, or if so what part is being played.

Tarabotti, for all her determined ambition as a writer, was disappointed by life and overflowing with a sense of griev-

ance, which in retrospect seems legitimate. Lame, like her father, she was placed in a convent at the age of eleven and
took her first vows at sixteen. Like Pallavicino, she was an in-
voluntary member of a religious order, in her case a victim
of monachization by force. Letizia Panizza describes *Paternal
Tyranny* as "predominantly an invective against the oppres-
sions of patriarchy; but it is also a treatise on the evils of
forcing young girls into a life they are not suited for, a psychological autobiography on the torments of childhood and
adolescence in the Venetian family of her day, a confession to
God of a soul's suffering, a literary critique of major texts of
contemporary misogyny, a feminist commentary on the Bible, and finally, the first manifesto about women's inalienable
rights to liberty, equality, and universal education."[41] If the
Incogniti can be considered to have thought, a hundred years
early, like the philosophes, Tarabotti thought like a feminist
two hundred years avant la lettre. She was the avenging angel
of oppressed young women whose lives were made unhappy
by paternal whim. Although she respected her vows, she rebelled by refusing to cut her hair or wear the habit of her order, and she transformed her personal fury into a polemical
indictment of the dirty deal between miserly fathers who
wanted to save money on a dowry and the readiness of the
Church to accept the vows of young nuns who lacked a vocation. "For these depraved fathers who sail the seas of the
world blown by passions inimical to salvation, convents take
the place of a ship's bilge, where they cast all their filthy re-
fuse and then boast of having offered up a sacrifice—even to

the point of adorning the brows of illegitimate daughters, often born of adulterous liaisons, with holy veils." Besides bastards, these fathers offered Christ "the most repulsive and deformed: lame, hunchbacked, crippled, or simple-minded. They are blamed for whatever natural defect they are born with and condemned to lifelong prison."[42]

Tarabotti even trespassed where no member of the Incogniti dared or wanted to go, by directly criticizing the Venetian government and the social system that sustained it. She recognized that her personal situation and that of other young women forced into convents in Venice were the consequence not just of paternal tyranny but of a deeper form of social oppression that masked itself as liberty. She noted how throughout the world no city had had a higher reputation for granting unconditional liberty to all its inhabitants, including even Jews. From its very beginning, however, the noble lords of Venice had embraced the "infernal monster of Paternal Tyranny."

> This [book] *Paternal Tyranny* is a gift that well suits a Republic that practices the abuse of forcing more young girls to take the veil than anywhere else in the world. . . . It is fair . . . to dedicate my book to your great senate and its senators, who, by imprisoning their young maidens so they chant the Psalter, pray, and do penance in their stead, hope to make you eternal, most beautiful virgin Republic, Queen of the Adriatic. . . . I shall not wheedle you into finding excuses for me, nor inveigle you into believing my sincerity. In any case,

once you have lost liberty, there remains nothing else to
lose.[43]

The title and the scathing introduction to *Paternal Tyranny*
made it impossible for Tarabotti to publish the book. She
was forced to change the title and write a new introduction
addressed to God and the Reader, rather than to Venice. As
Letizia Panizza notes, the change of title from *Paternal Tyranny* to *Innocence Betrayed* shifted attention from a critique of
patriarchy to an exploration of "women as innocent victims
whose destiny it is to suffer." More precisely than anyone else
at the time, Tarabotti unmasked the irony of Venetian propa-
ganda about republican liberty and identified the core con-
tradiction in Venetian society itself, the practice of restricted
marriage that led families to allow only one son per generation to marry and to keep their daughters off the marriage
market, most by removal to a nunnery. Tarabotti knew exactly what she was doing: "I realize that the subject matter is
scandalous because it goes against our political as well as
against our Catholic way of life." As open-minded as he was
in other respects and as supportive of the authorial ambi-
tions of the combative nun, Loredan remained an archcon-
servative when it came to the practice of restricted marriage,
no matter how painful the consequences for young women.
He had two sisters confined to convents and refused to support a young relative who wanted to marry rather than enter
a convent. He advised her, "You have been born noble, of a

distinguished family, but since you do not have a dowry to match your birth, you must either marry beneath you, or hazard the inconvenience of poverty. You will encounter universal contempt if you stain nobility with inferior alliances. . . . Those marriages are always unhappy where the partners are unequal by birth but equal in poverty."[44] Panizza suggests that Loredan had a role in suppressing the publication of *Paternal Tyranny* and *Convent Life as Hell,* and he certainly had the influence to have done so.

The libertine inclinations of the Incogniti, many of whom were, like Rocco and Pallavicino, renegade religious, built upon the skeptical reading of Aristotle that flourished in Padua while Cesare Cremonini was the dominant figure there. Unlike Cremonini, however, the Incogniti generation became obsessed with sexuality and gender roles. The Benedictine philosopher Antonio Rocco's defense of pederasty, the Lateranensi canon Ferrante Pallavicino's demented fascination with prostitutes, whom he reviled but whose wiles he could not escape, and the Benedictine nun Arcangela Tarabotti's anger over the lot of unwilling inmates of convents were all expressed in *novellas* and essays that were openly published in the relatively free environment of Venice or, in the case of the most controversial, were printed clandestinely or circulated privately in manuscript. The authors sometimes employed pen names; they publicly remained among the Unknowns, but everyone seemed to know who the authors really were. The singular literary obsession with sexuality, which appeared at a particular historical moment, the 1630s, '40s, and '50s, was a symptom of the disintegration of the Venetian aristocratic marriage and family life. By the 1640s a large part of the Venetian aristocracy had committed demographic suicide by failing to reproduce itself.

"Divorce" is an apt metaphor for this strange historical moment when the social foundations of the aristocracy fell apart. Not only did Christ seek to divorce the Roman Church, as in Pallavicino's allegory, but marriage itself became divorced from normal social practice and monogamous morality from the possibilities of life in Catholic Italy.

One day during the 1640s a gentleman masked for Carnival arrived in Sister Tarabotti's convent to pay homage to the literary star. He was none other than the most accomplished librettist in Venice, Giovanni Francesco Busenello. He was the author of *L'Incoronazione di Poppea,* an opera in which the emperor Nero arranged for the death of the Stoic philosopher Seneca. At the end of the opera, Nero crowns his adulterous lover empress of Rome. In Busenello's masterpiece, set to music by Claudio Monteverdi, the despised loose woman of Pallavicino's satire realizes the ultimate fantasy of love and acceptance. The collapse of Venetian aristocratic marriage meant that in the opera boxes numerous courtesans must have been able to identify with the fantasy of Poppea's good fortune. In the opera house the libertine impulses of the Incogniti created the most thorough commentary on the Venetian divorce between marriage and sexuality.

THREE

The Librettists

POPPEA IN THE
OPERA BOX

WHILE Ferrante Pallavicino languished in the pope's prison, thus missing the 1642–43 Venetian opera season, Giovanni Grimani's theater at San Giovanni e Paolo presented what has become perhaps the most notorious and certainly the most lasting work among early operas. With a libretto by that renowned member of the Accademia degli Incogniti Giovanni Francesco Busenello, and music (or at least most of it) by the venerable Claudio Monteverdi, *L'Incoronazione di Poppea* was the first opera based on historical events, in this case a story drawn from Cornelius Tacitus's *Annals* of the emperor Nero. Busenello's plot altered a story well known to at least some of the audience. The librettist's *argomento* lays out the plot, which is an inversion of the courtly love ethic:

Nero, in love with Poppaea, wife of Otho, as a pretext sent Otho as ambassador to Lusitania so that he could take his pleasure with her—this according to Cornelius Tacitus. But here facts are represented differently. Otho, deprived of Poppaea, gives himself over to delirium and exclamations. Octavia, wife of Nero, orders Otho to kill Poppaea. Otho promises to do it; but lacking the spirit to deprive his adored Poppaea of life, he dresses in the clothes of Drusilla, who was in love with him. Thus disguised, he enters the garden of Poppaea. Cupid awakens her, and prevents her death. Nero repudiates Octavia, in spite of the counsel of Seneca, and takes Poppaea to wife. Seneca dies and Octavia is banished from Rome.[1]

This constricted plot outline, the sort of thing one still reads in programs passed out in opera houses, hardly captures the allure and shock of the actual opera, especially as it came to be performed in a revised version after that first season. An exquisite final scene was added, by a composer whose identity is still debated among musicologists.[2] After Nero has forced Seneca to commit suicide and banished his frigid and infertile ("infrigidita ed infecunda") wife Ottavia from Rome, Nero marries the degraded Poppea and has her crowned empress. The opera ends with the best-known music in the opera, the love duet between Nero and Poppea,

> Pur ti miro, pur ti godo,
> Pur ti stringo, pur t'annodo
> Più non peno, più non moro,
> O mia vita, o mio tesoro.[3]

Oh, I desire you. Oh, I love you.
I embrace you, so I may keep you.
No more suffering, no more pain,
O my life, oh, my treasure.

Even by twenty-first-century standards, the immorality of
the ending is shocking. A murderous emperor and scheming
adulterous woman—a whore, in Venetian parlance—bring
down the curtain with a lyrical celebration of the power of
love.[4] Is this the triumph of love or lust? Does the opera admit to the possibility of a difference between them? Are the
success of Poppea's intrigues and the futility of Seneca's reason to be taken at face value or as a warning about the dangers of sensual indulgence?

The immorality of *Poppea* has created problems having to
do with its interpretation and especially an assessment of
how seventeenth-century Venetian audiences might have understood it.[5] One solution is to postulate that the story is not
what it appears to be. Iain Fenlon and Peter Miller have argued that the opera is marked by irony: "Indeed, a common
device in the opera is that meaning is the opposite of what
the music at first appears to be saying."[6] It may be a curious
interpretive move to assert that things are the opposite of
what they appear to be, but the reading is not entirely out of
keeping with the taste for paradox and the distrust characteristic of the members of the Incogniti, such as Busenello, of
the potential of language to convey precise meaning. By understanding the libretto in the light of contemporary Vene-

tian concepts of history, which owed much to Tacitus and his view that the appearances surrounding events had to be penetrated in order for the deeper meaning to emerge, Fenlon and Miller argue that contemporary Venetian audiences would have been aware of the rest of the story: Nero would later kick Poppea to death while she was pregnant with their child. These critics assume that Venetian audiences held as part of their common culture the historical knowledge that would have made them aware of "the illusory character of this seeming Triumph of Love."[7] Read this way, *Poppea* becomes a philosophical tract on the superiority of stoic virtues, but stoicism is not very sexy.[8] "Such a dull-witted morality play," as Susan McClary commented about the Fenlon-Miller interpretation, is not one likely to have appealed to audiences then or now.[9]

In contrast, Wendy Heller concentrates on the character that should stand most solidly for conventional morality, the spurned wife Ottavia. Heller argues,

> Listeners in the twenty-first century . . . want to believe that Love would weep for Ottavia rather than fight for Poppea; we want to applaud the institution of marriage, to condemn immoral sensuality, to enjoy the happy ending, to believe in Ottavia's sweet, unvengeful nature, or, at the very least, to revel in her stoic acceptance of a tragic fate. Yet . . . this is not an opera that endorses any of these more conventional virtues or upholds, in the characterization of Ottavia, a more unambiguous view of female suffering. Instead, we are left with a world in which singing is linked to sexual plea-

The story of Nero forcing the Stoic philosopher Seneca to commit suicide was a popular theme in the seventeenth century. Depicting the story was a way of critiquing the suffering of contemporary philosophers at the hands of authority, especially in Catholic Europe. Luca Giordano, *The Death of Seneca*. Louvre, Paris.

sure. Ottavia, with her unappealing chastity and condemnation of female existence, left out of the erotic triangle, is ex-
iled not only physically but also musically and left to die
under ambiguous circumstances. At the conclusion of the
opera, it is Poppea's sensuality that commands the stage.[10]

Heller's interpretation has the advantage, first of all, because it acknowledges the power of sexuality, but also because it comes closer to conveying the carnivalesque character
of early Venetian operatic theater, the fascination of contemporaries with women on the stage and with the sensuous
capacity of the female voice, and most of all the peculiar
composition of the Venetian audience. Who, after all, was
listening in all those opera boxes? I would suggest that there
were hardly any Ottavias but plenty of Poppeas—Venetian
courtesans or at least women whose connection to their
male companions was irregular—and in fact they must have
been there simply because so few Venetian patricians, male
or female, were married in the 1640s. As Heller has shown,
seventeenth-century Venetian opera displayed an abiding fascination with prostitutes and female sexuality, manifest most
graphically in the stories of Poppea and Messalina, a fascination that faded in the eighteenth century. Venetian opera
came to maturity at a moment when the practice of restricted
marriage for patrician men and monachization by force for
patrician women left most upper-class members of society
out of the marriage market. Venice had become the world of
the "single self," of persons who defined their social status
and their sexuality outside of the bonds of marriage.[11] For

many men extramarital liaisons were the norm; as a result, seventeenth-century Venice developed what Laura McGough has termed a thriving sexual economy, which produced not just numerous courtesans but many informal relationships and a network of social institutions created to provide social welfare for retired prostitutes and cast-off mistresses.[12] It was precisely at the moment when *Poppea* first appeared on the operatic stage that the full implications of the Venetian marriage market had become obvious. With the production of *Poppea,* the opera box became a model of the opera stage, where the relation between lust and love, sex and marriage, personal fulfillment and stoic suffering were very much thrown into question.

The masked occupants of the opera boxes were temporarily escaping from one of the most rigid marital regimes known to history. Since at least 1422 the Venetian patriciate had attempted to impose on its members a rigorous endogamy that prevented noble men from marrying women from outside the patriciate. The 1422 law of the Great Council denied membership in the nobility to sons born to noble fathers and mothers of lesser status. In 1506 the Council of Ten instituted the Libro d'Oro to register male noble births as a mechanism for disqualifying sons born to lower-class women, thereby protecting the Great Council from "contamination, blemishing, or any other denigration." By 1526 the burden of proof moved from birth registers of noble sons to marriage registers that provided evidence of the nobility of both husband and wife. Besides barring bastards and sons of non-noble mothers from the privileges of noble status, the new laws imposed a formal civil marriage procedure on the members of the ruling class. Thus, determining parentage on both sides became the means for guaranteeing endogamy within the ruling class.[13]

The consequence of Venetian marriage practices was thus the systematic production of patrician bachelors and patrician nuns. During the fifteenth century about half the male nobles who lived to adulthood remained bachelors. Some voluntarily chose celibacy, whether within the Church or without, and others were drawn to homoerotic relationships, but most seem to have had little choice whether to marry or not.[14] By the middle of the sixteenth century the combination of dowry inflation, which discouraged many patrician fathers from undertaking the expense of marrying their daughters, and price inflation, which eroded patrimonies, encouraged the practice of restricted marriage: families limited the number of children allowed to marry in order to prevent dispersal of the patrimony. There existed both a financial and a political logic to marriage restriction. In the absence of primogeniture laws, an inheritance had to be shared among all legitimate male offspring in each generation, and a partible inheritance became a diminished inheritance. For those seeking political alliances through marriage, a potential groom whose brothers did not marry would not be distracted by other affinal connections and could give his full support to his own in-laws, especially when it came to election to lucrative offices.[15] The officially unmarried brothers entered the sexual economy of Venice on their own terms through liaisons with male lovers, mistresses, prostitutes, courtesans, or secret marriages with lower-class women.

The same pressures that forced brothers to become bachelors drove an even higher percentage of their sisters into convents, whether they had a vocation or not. Throughout Italy between 1550 and 1650 the mushrooming monachization rates meant that aristocratic women everywhere were more likely to become nuns than wives. In Venice the increase was particularly dramatic: in 1581 nearly 54 percent of patrician women were nuns, and by the 1642–43 opera season, when *Poppea* was first produced, 82 percent may have become nuns, although this figure seems inflated.[16] A conservative estimate might be that during the late sixteenth and early seventeenth centuries about 60 percent of Venetian patrician women could be found in convents. Jutta Gisela Sperling demonstrates how the pressures of the dowry system and restricted marriage practices played out differently for women than for men. Even when blocked from marrying women of their own class, patrician men had access to the sexual economy or could marry secretly. In a sample of mid-seventeenth-century secret marriages registered in the Venetian curia, some 35 percent were between noblemen and women of lower class, but there is only one example of a noblewoman marrying a commoner. Unmarried patrician women were denied access to both the sexual economy and clandestine marriage opportunities.[17] Their fertility and their lives were squandered. In-

voluntary nuns were condemned to the hell of convent im-
prisonment, unpurged of their sensual desires despite their
chaste marriage to Christ, as the otherwise antagonistic writers Arcangela Tarabotti and Ferrante Pallavicino both recognized.

The results were a tragic waste of human potential—un-
bridled sexual exploitation of lower-class women by noblemen; frustration and anger among the nuns deprived of pleasure and fulfillment in life; and the demographic suicide of
the Venetian ruling class. Matters reached a breaking point
just three years after *Poppea*'s debut. In 1646 and again in 1669,
the Venetian patriciate had to sell itself, by offering titles of
nobility for the price of 100,000 ducats, in order to provide
enough new men to fill political offices and to finance the
Turkish wars.[18] The very endogamous strategy the patriciate
had devised in the fifteenth century to prevent pollution
from below had bled it of vigor by the seventeenth and made
class pollution the only alternative that would allow survival.

The suitability of opera as a commentary on the harsh divorce between marriage and sexuality in Venice derived from
its connections with Carnival, the season when the theaters
were opened and operas produced. Opera owed as much to
the traditions of Venetian theater and carnival culture, which
had long provided a critique of the city's peculiar sexual
economy, as it did to the musical ideas of the Florentine theorists of opera. At the end of the sixteenth century the
Camerata theorists under Medici patronage invented a form

of musical drama now called opera for performance in the courtly environment of the Grand Duchy of Tuscany.[19] One of the late sixteenth-century Florentine musical theorists was none other than Galileo Galilei's father, Vincenzo, who wrote what "is surely the most influential music treatise of the late sixteenth century."[20] Vincenzo Galilei was a lutenist and ardent advocate of the revival of Greek monody to replace modern polyphony and counterpoint. "The key to the power of ancient music was the solitary melody, the single 'air,' however many were singing together. Even animals exploit the voice, a natural instrument for expressing their feelings and wants. Yet some rational animals—that is modern composers and theorists—neglect this resource as a means of expressing human passions."[21] Vincenzo Galilei and his Camerata colleagues' theory of monody became the founding principle of what became opera. The new musical drama was further elaborated in Rome, but it was only with the introduction in Venice of opera theaters that catered to a paying public that ponderous courtly spectacles mutated into the lively popular art that opera has remained for the past four hundred years. With the opening of the Teatro San Cassiano in 1637, "opera as we know it," in the words of Ellen Rosand, "assumed its definitive identity—as a mixed theatrical spectacle available to a socially diversified, and paying, audience; a public art."[22] *L'Incoronazione di Poppea* was the twenty-fourth new opera presented in Venice during the six years that followed the first production of 1637, and by 1645 thirty-five different operas had been produced, evidence of a remarkable cultural moment of intense creativity and of the competition for audiences.[23]

Why did this efflorescence take place in Venice, and why then? Why did opera first succeed as a public art in Venice between 1637 and 1645, by which date all the elements of the new form were fully evident? The answer, I would argue, is not to be found so much in the aesthetics of operatic music, no matter how great the compositions of Monteverdi, Cavalli, and the other masters of that formative operatic period, even if the music is what has made opera last. As James H. Johnson has put it in reference to ancien régime Paris, opera was a social duty: "Attending the opera was more a social event than aesthetic encounter."[24] In Venice owning or renting an opera box was the privilege of the upper levels of the Venetian patriciate, of visiting aristocrats or royalty, and (significantly) of foreign ambassadors. Because the access that foreign ambassadors had to Venetian policy makers was carefully controlled by law, attendance at the opera became one of the rare opportunities ambassadors had to see and be seen, to pick up gossip, and even to enjoy a moment of private conversation with a Venetian senator or procurator in the dark recesses of an opera box. In 1672 the English resident, John Dodington, requested that the doge bestow on him boxes in two separate theaters, but Dodington readily admitted, "I do not ask for them for my own satisfaction or taste, seeing, as I declare, that I do not love music. As regards poetry, I do not esteem it, and I do not understand the theater. The only reason I ask for this favor is so that I might keep up appearances: my most recent predecessor had boxes, and all the other residents currently at this court have them."[25]

The answer about why Venice and why then is to be found, it would seem, in the conjunction of Venetian carnival festivity and the intellectual politics of late-Renaissance culture wars. The extraordinary period during the early seventeenth century of relatively free speech and cultural creativity, by comparison with what was possible elsewhere in Italy at the same time, was made possible by the banishment of the Society of Jesus from Venetian territories between 1606 and 1657. In Venice wandering aristocrats, displaced priests, renegade monks, and speculative thinkers found aid and comfort in the intellectual politics of the Venetian academies whose members wrote the libretti and financed the theaters for many of the early Venetian operas. Ellen Rosand has suggested that only in Venice did three conditions prevail that made the permanent establishment of opera possible: "regular demand, dependable financial backing, and a broad and predictable audience."[26] Early Venetian opera certainly had spectacular success in drawing audiences and tourists to Venice, but opera was then, as now, seldom a profitable commercial investment. Even though property owners built new theaters, impresarios invested capital in new productions, and librettists, composers, set designers, musicians, and singers ventured their livelihoods in a risky enterprise, early opera, as far as I can tell, was a financial loser. From the very beginning opera needed help. Requiring patrons to sustain it, it was only superficially a commercial enterprise.[27] Why, then, were some people more than willing to foot the bill?

Many of those who did supply funding were notorious libertines, and opera—despite its claims to being "serious," as opposed to comic, theater—was from the beginning completely implicated in the bacchanalian behavior of Venetian Carnival. A certain paradox is in evidence here, because it was the public nature of the opera houses that made true privacy possible, especially by contrast with princely courts, at which the prince was the ultimate patron, acknowledged by everyone. In public theaters patrons could disguise their true identities or at least avoid full responsibility for what appeared on stage. As mentioned earlier, they were quite literally unknowns, Incogniti. The carnival seasons of the 1630s and 1640s in Venice offered a singular opportunity for "unknowns" to indulge in theatrical experimentation on an unprecedented scale. Of course, because it was the carnival season, the audience members were themselves masked, at least when they arrived, and thus unknown patrons staged for the unknowns in the opera boxes productions that took advantage of the collective anonymity. The opera theater became a stage for all the paradoxes of a society structured around the arts of dissimulation. Audience members came to be "seen" and to see others, at the same time as they dissimulated their real identity by wearing masks. The theaters arranged the private boxes in such a way that each became a "miniature stage" visible to at least some of the others, and one of the innovations of opera houses was that the very shape of the box mirrored the configuration of the proscenium.[28] The great dramatic achievement of Venetian opera was to employ music and spectacle to warm the spirits of members of polite society schooled in the cool habits of dissimulation, by appealing directly to human feeling and thus uncovering true emotions, if not true identities.

The history of early opera belongs perhaps more to the history of carnivalesque drama than of music. At first *opera lirica* was merely dramas with music, or more graphically, "poetry clothed in music."[29] The librettist was king, and libretti were frequently published at the time the opera was performed, whereas composers seemed to be virtually interchangeable, and most of the scores are now lost, perhaps because they were considered ephemera. Carnival occasioned ribald and often satirical comedies performed during the annual season of festive license, and the connection to Carnival created an ambiguous relationship with the forces of authority in Venice. The history of Venetian theater betrays a recurrent dialectic between the licentious behavior of the "popular" and youthful (often patrician youth), on the one hand, and the authoritarian impulse for social control of the elderly patrician officeholders, on the other. As early as 1508 the Council of Ten prohibited unauthorized private and public theatrical performances at Carnival and weddings, especially those employing comedians and buffoons in masks who engaged in mime and exaggerated elocution.[30] From the mid-fifteenth to the late sixteenth centuries, theatrical entertainments for Carnival and those for special occasions, such as visits of princes and ambassadors, triumphal entries, and weddings, tended to be organized and financed by the *compagnie della calza*, which were festive clubs of young nobles known for their hedonism and for pushing the limits of their elders' tolerance.[31] The companies protected their members from official heat through a code of silence: the statutes of at least three of the companies had provisions stating, "Each member must keep secret the affairs of the company."[32] As Linda Carroll has shown, the hired performers, especially the most famous early comic playwright, the Paduan known as Ruzante, suffered official displeasure when matters went too far.[33] Ruzante employed peasant characters to satirize and sometimes bitterly criticize the pretension of the upper classes, and under the protection of his young patrons he pushed the limits of toleration. The diarist Marino Sanuto described one of these occasions: "Ruzante and Menato, Paduan peasants, performed a rustic comedy and it was completely lascivious, with very dirty words, and God was blasphemed by all of them, and the [audience] shrieked at them."[34] After Ruzante apparently insulted the French ambassador, even his young protectors could not save him, and he never appeared on the Venetian stage again.

The Council of Ten's 1508 licensing requirement for comic theater was never abrogated but, like so many Venetian laws, was only selectively enforced. Official displeasure, however, did tend to drive comic theater out of the public *piazzetta* and *campi* where it had been performed on outdoor stages, into private courtyards that could be closed off and transformed into temporary theaters. By around 1580, as Eugene J. Johnson has shown, patrician entrepreneurs had constructed two commercial theaters in Venice for performances by commedia dell'arte troupes. The inclusion in these theaters of boxes rented out to the public made them prototypes for the *teatro all'italiana*, the Italian opera house form that spread across Europe after the initial success of opera in seventeenth-century Venice. Although their exact location is unknown, both theaters were in the parish of San Cassiano, one owned by the Michiel family and the other by the Tron, whose theater in San Cassiano in 1637 was the first one used for opera. The distinguishing feature of these theaters, especially by comparison with the open seating plan of the Teatro Olimpico in Vicenza, was the inclusion of several stories' worth of boxes that provided elevated, separated, private spaces from which paying customers, presumably patricians and distinguished foreigners, could watch performances. Johnson suggests that the theater box may have originated in the Venetian tradition of using windows and balconies, such as those of the Procuratie Vecchie and the Marciana Library, as private spaces for viewing public events, such as ducal processions and carnival festivities. As Johnson puts it, "the theater boxes created a novel social space, simultaneously private and public—or, one might say, private in places of public access. Apparently, Venetians quickly figured out how to use these rather cramped *palchi* as if they were modern motel rooms; this behavior brought on a vigorous reaction from the Council of Ten."[35] And as with motel rooms, it is probably less important what actually took place in those closed little spaces than what contemporaries imagined was taking place. The Venetian theater box itself became a stage for the imagination and a metaphor for the libertine life.

The reaction to the presumed activities in the *palchi* was immediate. The Florentine ambassador to Venice wrote in 1581 in a letter, "It is maintained that the Jesuit priests have complained a great deal that in the boxes that have been erected in these two places many wicked acts take place creating scandal."[36] The scandal was that gentlemen were apparently using the boxes for assignations with courtesans. In the Sant' Aponal opera house during the mid-seventeenth century, the box closest to the proscenium at stage right was reserved "per le donne," presumably courtesans, a fact that hints at a Venetian tradition of cavorting with or at least making connections with courtesans in theater and opera boxes.[37] Because the early Venetian theaters presented obscene comedies in a venue where obscene acts were taking place on the other side of the thin walls of the wooden boxes, Venetian theater life was indeed rife with scandal.

At first, attempts to clean up the theaters were indirect. The Jesuits and their allies on the Council of Ten argued that the danger from fire or collapse in the wooden theaters was too great, and in 1580, the Ten required that no comedy be presented "until first there be sworn statements from architects and specialists, who will be sent by the heads of this council diligently to inspect the places where the performances will be given, that they are strong and secure, so that no ruin may happen there."[38] In 1581 the Ten passed a decree that seemed to permit young patricians to perform comedies but banned professional actors. The following carnival season, a minority among the Ten attempted to pass a decree to open up the scandalous boxes, "so that everyone who passes by can see inside these boxes, and thus they must stay open for all these fifteen days." An additional decree that failed to pass attempted to light up all the dark corners by ordering "that lamps be placed in all the corridors before the performances of the comedies and kept lit until they are over and everyone has left the place where they are performed."[39] The restrictions the Council of Ten placed on the two theaters for comedy performances escalated. Finally, the theaters were forced to close, and in 1585 the Ten ordered them torn down.

Writing in 1607, Antonio Persio, whose patron was Zaccaria Contarini, the head of the Ten when it ordered the dismantling of the theaters, credited the Jesuit fathers with agitating successfully for the destruction of the theaters. Persio's account appeared in a manuscript written in defense of the papal cause during the Venetian Interdict of 1606–1607. Persio criticized the Venetians, whom he called the *veneriani* rather than *venetiani*, for their addiction to avarice and *luxuria*. His two examples of Venetian *luxuria* were the theaters and the plunging necklines of Venetian women who attended the theater. In his account the Jesuits had corrected the Venetians by having their theaters destroyed and the breasts of their women covered.[40] However, the interdict crisis put an end to the direct influence of the Jesuits. The banishment of the Society of Jesus, by eliminating the most vociferous anti-theater lobby, opened the way for the return of seasonal public theater, as opposed to occasional clandestine, comic theater. The Tron reconstructed its theater at San Cassiano for the performance of comedies, and it was in a rebuilt version of this famous theater that the first public performance of an opera for a paying audience took place during Carnival in 1637.

Long before that first operatic performance, Venetians thus had a well-established tradition that associated Carnival, comedy, courtesans, theaters, and scandal. At the same time, the intellectual politics of Venice remained firmly conservative and committed to a patriotic consensus devoted to republicanism, but within that consensus profound intellectual disagreements divided the ruling nobility, disagreements that were often brought to the surface by the influence of the Jesuits on Venetian public life. Even in 1652 during the War of Candia, when Venice desperately needed military support from the papacy, some fifty-three senators still voted against allowing the Jesuits to return.[41] The banishment of Jesuits, however, had created opportunities for two generations of seriously playful, mostly young intellectuals, some of whom had libertine inclinations, and it was these nobles and their foreign friends who promoted and supported early Venetian opera.[42] The first opera in Venice was produced by Benedetto Ferrari and Francesco Manelli's traveling company of musicians, which had performed another opera the previous season in Padua. Padua incubated a host of innovations in Venetian intellectual life, which, as we have seen, was sustained in the lagoon city by the academies.[43]

The Accademia degli Incogniti did not invent Venetian opera, but the influence of its members on the new art form can hardly be overstated. In 1640 the Incogniti inspired the construction of a brand-new building, the Teatro Novissimo, the fourth opera house to open in Venice. The Novissimo was committed to producing only heroic operas with music, rather than comic plays, and although it presented only six operas during its short life span of five years, these established a distinctive Venetian operatic tradition. The Novissimo brought together professional musicians from Rome with the learned Venetian academicians who had articulated the theory of opera and produced the libretti for the new productions. Although several of the Incogniti had been active in opera from the time of the earliest productions in Venice, at the Novissimo the Incogniti worked as a group. They produced in 1641 what Rosand has called "the first and possibly the greatest operatic 'hit' of the century," *La finta Pazza* (The Fake Mad Woman), which set a standard for spectacular production, including machines, stage sets, costumes, and singing. With a libretto by the Incognito Giulio Strozzi (the stepfather of the angelic-voiced Barbara Strozzi), music by Francesco Sacrati, and stage sets by Giacomo Torelli (the engineer to the doge), and starring the first "prima donna," Anna Renzi, in the title role, *La finta Pazza* generated tremendous audience enthusiasm, especially because of the spectacular machines and sets. It also favored local Venetian tastes in its evocation of the myth of the Trojan origins of Venice and references to the contemporary Turkish wars, which brought ancient mythology up to the minute.[44]

At the Novissimo the Incogniti succeeded in realizing in practice what had been until then largely a theoretical justification for inserting music into a drama. Under Cremonini's influence, the Incogniti had debated the classical precedents for sung drama. It is unclear how much they knew about the sixteenth-century Florentine theorists of opera and the composers who staged in Florence and Rome the very first operas, which were noncommercial. However, Galileo's father, Vincenzo Galilei, was one of those theorists, as mentioned earlier, and his ideas were probably in circulation among the students at Padua who later founded the Incogniti. Whatever the case, the Venetians drew up their own arguments, which pointed to the various uses of music in ancient drama and to the ways in which their dramas resembled or differed from those of the ancients.[45] Unlike the Florentines, whose humanist educations had impelled them to theorize about the historical function of music in classical drama, the Venetians argued that in the end it did not really matter what the ancients had done. The Incogniti defended musical drama because it appealed to contemporary tastes. As Busenello, the librettist for *Poppea*, put it, "may those who enjoy enslaving themselves to the ancient rules find their fulfillment in baying at the full moon."[46]

During its first forty years, Venetian opera became the paramount contemporary art form. By 1678, nine theaters had been adapted or built for opera, and the essential elements were in place, including competition among opera houses; librettists, composers, singers, and set designers jumping from theater to theater; hits and flops; the cult of the diva; extensive publicity campaigns; season ticket holders; sold-out performances; claques for particular singers; and tourists who came to Venice just to hear operas during carnival season. As Rosand has shown, opera soon suffered from the Sisyphean consequences of success, because each season operagoers demanded new surprises and novelties. In 1650, a scant thirteen years after the first opera production in Venice, Pietro Paolo Bissari complained,

> The city of Venice, having enjoyed approximately fifty *opera regie* in only a few years, of which few cities have seen the like, and those only with difficulty, at a wedding or on some other solemn occasion of their princes, has rendered the authors sterile and nauseated the listeners, it having become difficult to come up with things not already seen, or to make them appear more effective, with greater spectacle and display, than they ever seemed before.[47]

With success, though, Venetian opera also became more specialized and professional. To keep up with demand, Venetian theaters had to rely on outside talent, musicians and singers brought in at the last moment, and as a result Venetian opera became less Venetian; Venice was a stop on the burgeoning opera circuit, as singers and composers moved from court to court and town to town. The rise of public

opera theaters in Venice, moreover, was just one manifestation of the Europewide transformation toward the commercialization of entertainment during the late sixteenth and
seventeenth centuries. In Venice itself, the famous bridge
battles, once a ritualized manifestation of popular culture
and working-class rivalries, had by the early seventeenth century come to be managed by patrician fight "fans," who gam-
bled on the outcome and tried to influence it by hiring the
best combatants. As Robert Davis has shown, in the bridge
battles one can trace the beginnings of the professionaliza-
tion and commercialization of sport.[48] In late sixteenth- and
early seventeenth-century Madrid and London, public theaters that supported such writers as Cervantes and Shakespeare came to be built, competed among themselves for audiences, thrived on novelty and scandal, and struggled with
the vicissitudes of commercial success and failure. In all these
examples, the commercialization of entertainment survived
through a hybrid system in which impresarios risked their
capital and artists, their talent and time, to produce entertainments that nevertheless still required patrons, who sometimes owned the theaters or who might intervene financially
to bail out productions. The motives of these patrons were
obscure and often private, perhaps ultimately unrecoverable
by historians. Some clearly had an intellectual agenda, others
a sense of noblesse oblige; and many certainly enjoyed the results of their patronage. Giovanni Morelli and Thomas R.
Walker have written that opera, "which achieved what princes
provided through generosity, in Venice, in no way inferior,

was produced through business."[49] The same could be said about the Globe in London or many other theaters of the period.

But why did opera, which had been a court entertainment for nearly forty years, suddenly catch on in Venice in 1637? The simple answer is that the opera performed the year before in Padua had attracted the attention and admiration of Venetian aristocrats, who were motivated to promote similar productions in Venice itself. It seems, though, that more was going on than simple emulation of a successful production, because the transition from comic drama to serious drama with music marked a significant shift in the taste of the theatergoing public. The seventeenth-century critic Cristoforo Ivanovich suggested that the devastating plague of 1630, which killed perhaps a third of the Venetian population, drew a line of demarcation through Venetian attitudes toward the theater. The appearance of plague had put the carnival season comedies in jeopardy, but when some visiting diplomats, whose home country's support was critical in the pending war against the Turks, requested that the comic performances go on, the Council of Ten threw caution to the wind and yielded to diplomatic exigencies. The Ten even authorized performances out of season to please visitors who had missed carnival season. These decisions confirmed the diplomatic and political role of Venetian public theater. For the next forty years comedies and, later, operas were integrated into the seasonal calendar of civic rituals. The new productions premiered soon after All Saints' Day and continued through the carnival season until Ash Wednesday. A second season opened after Ascension Day, when tourists came to Venice to watch the pageantry of the annual marriage of the sea ceremony, which since the thirteenth century had inaugurated the sailing season and drawn pilgrims bound for Jerusalem. After the Ottoman conquests curtailed pilgrimages, the less pious charms of Venice continued to lure visitors. Venice hosted a huge market for luxury goods on Ascension Day, which brought in foreign merchants, shoppers, and eventually pleasure-seeking tourists.[50]

The sense of relief that pervaded Venice after the 1630 plague reinforced the popularity of theater as a welcome divertissement from the fear of death, or at least so Carmelo Alberti has suggested. It seems improbable that one could prove or disprove this psychological hypothesis, but it does echo Giovanni Boccaccio's report in the introduction to the *Decameron* that some Florentines adopted a devil-may-care attitude after the Black Death of 1348. Certainly some comics on the Venetian stage "laughed at the vermin in the grave," thus leavening tragedy with comic relief.[51] The early operas, however, were not comedies, and in fact they probably represent a reaction to the decline in the dramatic quality of comic performances and a shift in aristocratic tastes during the decade of the 1630s. Crude comedies also lowered the social level of theater audiences, which by Ivanovich's report included "the vulgar." Some patricians proclaimed their desire for nobler entertainments. The opportunity for profits and the enthusiasm of aristocratic patrons led theater owners to respond to the shift in taste by producing operas rather than commedia dell'arte performances, which began to disappear from the Venetian stage.

Opera, given form by the nobles of the academies and their hired musicians, composers, and set designers, soon became the dominant theatrical genre in Venice. Thanks to their success, the spectacles of opera soon became "normal" entertainment, and in so doing began to lose their innovative spirit and to conform to the tried and true conventions that would yield predictable profits and provide an inoffensive occasion for social encounters. The notorious conclusion of Busenello's *L'Incoronazione di Poppea*, was, in fact, quite unusual in its openly libertine ethos. A decade and a half later, the Accademia degli Imperturbabili, which rented the Teatro Sant' Aponal in 1657 and whose members produced at least two libretti, offered a far less ambitious and scandalous theory of drama accompanied by music than had the Incogniti. The Imperturbabili proposed a safer, more modest program, "to pass, in honest and virtuous recreation, the most dangerous days of the year [that is, Carnival]."[52]

The commercialized culture of opera and opera houses became by the 1640s the most vital theatrical expression of the culture wars of the late Renaissance. Opera was rooted in late-Renaissance theories about the relationship between singing and emotional expression in ancient Greek music, but it was also a free-spirited form of expression utterly at odds with the theatrical ideas of the Society of Jesus, which had the most thoroughly articulated ideology about both the value and the dangers of drama. The Jesuits were touched by the same humanist influences as were the theorists of opera, but Jesuit views evolved in an entirely different direction, toward the creation of a distinctive Jesuit theater. In the Jesuit colleges, training in Latin eloquence was perfected through the recitation of "dialogues." As Ignatius put it, "In the schools, boys from all walks of life are to be accepted, provided they are willing to observe the required restraint and discipline; and to make things more interesting for them, and to afford them and their parents pleasure, at times during the year orations should be delivered, and verses and dialogues, as is done in Rome. This will also add to the prestige of the school."[53] The recitation of these simple dialogues was enormously successful, and they evolved into full-fledged plays that became an integral part of the academic and liturgical calendar of the colleges. In addition, the Jesuits conceived of acting as a form of methodical prayer, an imitation of Christ that had to be performed on a world stage in which the providential plan of God could be acted out not only for the guidance of Christians but also for the conversion of heathens. As Marc Fumaroli notes, "Ignatius is a directorial genius to be compared with Stanislawski or Brecht. . . . Jesuit college drama and ballet at their best are, within their erudite allegories, another and an outer form of spiritual exercises, rehearsing the anagogical and mystical drama of the divine Word at work in the labyrinthine world of human souls and actions, in order to return multiplicity to unity, disorder to order, anguish to joy."[54] Jesuit colleges employed theater for more than the edification of youth. Pastoral theater became the third front in the campaign for Jesuit prestige, as important as missions and the colleges themselves; and in cosmopolitan centers such as Lisbon, Jesuits dominated the urban stage.[55] During the early seventeenth century Jesuit theater was a major force for inculcating the values of post-Tridentine Catholicism virtually everywhere except Venice. It is probably no accident that commercial opera first thrived in the most important Catholic city without a Jesuit theatrical presence.

The rules of the Jesuit colleges incorporated theater into the curriculum. Plays were performed on prize day for students who had achieved honors in their studies and during Carnival when edifying comedies provided an alternative to the more lascivious entertainments that prevailed outside the college walls. Thus, Jesuit colleges produced at least two plays for the public every year, but there were plenty of special occasions for additional plays. "Tragedies and comedies must be in Latin, and they must be very few. Their subjects should be religious and edifying, and there should be no interludes that are not in Latin and in good taste. No female characters or costumes may be used."[56] In fact, no female spectators were to be allowed into the performances. On no issue did the Jesuits and Venetian musical theater differ more dramatically than on the role of women on stage. Whereas Venetian opera represented a celebration of female eroticism and men and women mingled freely in the opera audience, Jesuit dramatic theory supplied a harsh warning about the dangers of allowing women in the theater. Among religious the Jesuits were hardly alone in their cultivation of the theater as a form of pious expression. Italian nunneries had a thriving dramatic tradition that included spiritual comedies, and gender segregation also prevailed at their productions. All the actors were women, and as a rule the audience members were exclusively other nuns and secular women. Attendance by laymen and priests was the occasional exception to the rule.[57]

At least as far back as the early sixteenth century, women and men mixed together in the audiences for the comedies staged during Carnival. By about the 1540s women started to appear onstage alongside male actors. Isabella Andreini of Padua (b. 1562) attracted a considerable public following without apparent shame, becoming the first female "star" of the theater.[58] Nevertheless, the prejudice against women on stage persisted. For Christian moralists, justification for the prejudice could be found in the writings of Salvianus, a disciple of Augustine. Salvianus argued that audiences were as complicit in sin as actors because of the audience's desire to identify with dramatic characters: "The indecencies of the spectacles involve actors and audience in substantially the same guilt."[59] English Puritans asserted that playacting is inherently evil because the actor substitutes a contrived self for the "absolute identity" given by God. To pretend to be someone other than who God has ordained is to deny divine will. The Puritans' attack on theater paralleled their critique of the liturgy. True worship must directly translate the inner spiritual state of the worshipper and should not be mediated by ritual scripts, formulas, or prescribed gestures. In addition, there were the moral dangers that Jonas Barish has eloquently summarized:

> Clearly, the whole complex of theater, dance, music, gorgeous attire, luxurious diet, cosmetics, feminine seductiveness, feminine sexuality, transvestism, etc., aroused a painful anxiety in the foes of the stage, perhaps not only because it symbolized irrational forces threatening chaos, but because it represented a deeply disturbing temptation, which could only be dealt with by being disowned and converted into passionate moral outrage.[60]

The Puritan complaint about the insincerity of actors did not have much purchase in Catholic Italy, but Italian critics shared concerns about the moral dangers of the stage.

The scourge of Italian theater was the Jesuit Gian Domenico Ottonelli. Joseph Connors pictures Ottonelli as a "guerrilla engaged in combat against the theater and especially against the role of women in it."[61] The first evidence of Ottonelli has him closing down a comedy performance in Catania in 1635 because it contained a single obscene gesture. Obsessed with the presumed sexual promiscuity of actresses, Ottonelli employed a network of spies to attend and report on performances and further relied on the confessional to provide him with information. Noting that lecherous nobles had not infrequently raped famous actresses, the Jesuit demanded that women be excluded from the stage, not for their own protection but because they were "infernal Amazons," dressed up to look like someone other than who they were. The seduction of a woman's eyes especially troubled him, and he cited Aristotle as the source for the view that women's glances dispensed poison. Aware that women had been banned from the stage in England, Ottonelli considered recommending the English solution of dressing boys up to play the female parts, but he backed off because of the risk of encouraging pederasty. In the end, the most he found allowable in dramas was the sound of a woman's voice from offstage. Ottonelli had some success in driving women and obscene comedies from the stages of Palermo, Naples, and Florence, but he made little headway in the Rome of the Barberini, and as a Jesuit he certainly could not have preached in Venice against the seductive female voices of the opera stage.

At the core of the Jesuit conception of theater was the *imitatio Christi,* adoption of the outward role of an exemplary character as a way of inculcating inward spirituality. The Jesuit approach was theologically the opposite of the Calvinist-Puritan critique. For the Jesuits, therefore, the words of the script became more than exercises in Latin eloquence; they were quasi-liturgical, efficacious through their mere repetition, for actor and audience alike. The Jesuits emphasized the absolute power and meaning of words. Language was the medium of persuasion, for self-discovery, divine praise, and prayer. Whatever Ferrante Pallavicino had asserted in *The Rhetoric of Whores* about the dissimulation inherent in Jesuit rhetorical practices, the Jesuits themselves employed rhetoric to persuade for the good and to interpret the meaning of God's Word. The actor became the mouthpiece of God.

Seventeenth-century Venetian opera, however, tended in the opposite direction, toward dissociation of meaning and voice. As one early eighteenth-century critic put it, "what is left in the theaters is only pure voice, stripped of any poetic eloquence and of any philosophical feeling."[62] Mauro Calcagno has analyzed the asynchronicity between the semiotics of music and those of language, as they "'slide' for a moment over each other," creating the dramatically engaging quality in Venetian opera—the "oscillation between associating and dissociating music and verbal meaning."[63] He notes how the aesthetic justification for the disjuncture between music and text derived from the recurring tropes of nothingness and the singing of the nightingale in the works of the Incognito thinkers, the ancient notion of the song sung for its own sake. These tropes came to be associated with the pure voice of a woman singing long melismatic passages utterly disconnected from the text of the libretto, a practice that led to the musical, lyrical, and emotional excesses so characteristic of early opera. The Incognito trope of nothingness was celebrated in *The Glories of Nothing*, written by Marin Dall'Angelo and published in a collection of discourses delivered at meetings of the Incogniti.[64]

The trope revealed a certain discontent with the limits of Renaissance modes of expression and doubt about the capacity of the arts to imitate nature.[65] The profound rhetorical

skepticism of the Incogniti, which was rooted in the philosophical skepticism of Cremonini, eroded confidence in artistic norms and rules and led the librettists and composers
of opera to seek artistic forms free of constraint that would
enable them to privilege creativity, spontaneity, and emotional expression over the representational burden of language. As Calcagno asks, "why bother to musically reflect the
meaning of words if they signify nothing?" The answer was
to be found in opera: "Distrust of the meaning of language
is compensated by trust in the power of voice."[66] At the moment of pure song, sung by a seductive female voice—and
by extension a woman uncontrolled and uncontrollable, a
woman without a tether to meaning but only to the emotion
of the moment, a pure, divine *pazza*—Venetian opera, which
carried operatic concepts to the other European capitals,
brought the Renaissance to an end. The Renaissance project
of developing rhetoric and musical theory to create an art
that imitated nature, according to the principle of verisimili-
tude, fell apart in the Incognito discourses and libretti. These
depicted the world as being not so much without meaning as
divorced from nature—divorced as Venetian sexual life was
from monogamous marriage. Song helped ground people
emotionally, amid the disorientation produced by a culture
built on extreme social restrictions.

The opera stage was a model for the opera box, in the
sense that the box was as much a stage as the stage itself.[67]
The relationship between singers and the audience, of course,

could hardly be a simple or even a single one. The processes of artistic novelty and suggestibility were too indirect for it to be straightforward, and the traditions of carnival celebrations encouraged a considerable degree of give and take between the performers and the audience. The dynamic in question clearly went far beyond identification with a character, especially in opera where language evanesces in favor of pure voice. The correspondence between box and stage became so powerful in Venice, I suggest, because the actual experience of social and sexual life at the time was itself so completely divorced from the language of Christian morality. Opera created a miniature or model of an all-too-common experience and offered a way of escaping the dissimulations required by polite society. Song became the medium for penetrating behind the masks and calculated self-presentations of the Venetian audiences, to stir their inner passions.

Who then was that masked *donna* in the opera box, the occasional companion of an aristocratic box holder? The masks of Carnival and the duplicity of polite society meant, of course, that the answer remains a secret. That is the whole point. Only the Nero onstage married his lover, crowned her empress, and sang, "Oh, I desire you. Oh, I love you. / I embrace you, so I may keep you." But to imagine such things, perhaps only for a brief moment, does not seem unwarranted for those trapped in the prison of Venetian marital structures. The deepest tragedy lies in the fate of all those nuns, immured in the bleaker prison and unable to see their fantasies played out on an opera stage.

In 1657 the Jesuits returned to Venice. During the Thirty Years' War (1618–1648) Venice had lost its most lucrative markets in Germany, and the Cretan War (1645–1669) created a terrible financial drain on the public coffers.[68] Venice desperately needed papal support against the Turks, and the price they paid was to invite the Jesuits to reestablish their presence in the Venetian dominion. The consequences for the operatic stage were soon felt, as a more conservative cultural atmosphere made impresarios cautious. The patrician families associated with the Jesuits gained the upper hand in the Senate, and prominent families such as the Grimani, the very ones who had staged *L'Incoronazione di Poppea* in their theater, became concerned about how patronage of the arts might mar their public image. The abrupt cancellation of Francesco Cavalli's *Eliogabalo*, scheduled for the 1667–68 season at the Grimani theater, seems to have been a direct consequence of the revival of Jesuit influence in Venice.[69] The culture wars that had begun in 1591 with the student riots against the Jesuit college in Padua ended with a mad scramble to rewrite an opera libretto to conform to the reigning religious and ethical sensibility, a sensibility at odds with the vaunted liberty of Venice, which had for so long supplied the first line of Catholic defense against the Turks. No longer a great naval power, Venice was now becoming a stop on the itinerary of courtesan-seeking, operagoing tourists. The city finally had to admit that it needed the support of the pope more than it needed the subtleties of the Incogniti, who had stopped meeting after the death of Loredan in 1661.[70] With the demise of the Incogniti the Renaissance project had come to an end, but the waning years of the Renaissance left a lasting legacy of philosophical skepticism, scientific materialism, and literary libertinism, along with the thrill of all those passionate voices singing on the opera stage.

Notes · Index

Notes

Introduction

1. William J. Bouwsma, *The Waning of the Renaissance, 1550–1640* (New Haven, Conn., 2000), 1.
2. John Jeffries Martin, *Myths of Renaissance Individualism* (Houndmills, U.K., 2004).
3. Virginia Cox, "The Single Self: Feminist Thought and the Marriage Market in Early Modern Venice," *Renaissance Quarterly* 48 (1995): 513–576.
4. Valeria Finucci and Regina Schwartz, eds., *Desire in the Renaissance: Psychoanalysis and Literature* (Princeton, 1994).
5. Bouwsma, *The Waning of the Renaissance*, 112–113.

1. The Skeptics

1. Bertolt Brecht, *The Life of Galileo*, trans. Desmond I. Vesey (London, 1960), 28 (act 1, scene 1).

2. Ibid., 50–55.
3. Galileo Galilei, *Le Opere* (Florence, 1901), vol. ii, letter no. 564, p. 165. All translations are mine unless otherwise noted.
4. On Cremonini's career, Charles B. Schmitt, "Cesare Cremonini, un Aristotelico al tempo di Galilei," *Centro Tedesco di Studi Veneziani, Quaderni* 16 (1980): 3–21.
5. Luigi Lazzerini, "Le radici folkloriche dell'anatomia: Scienza e rituale all'inizio dell'età moderna," *Quaderni storici* 85 (1994): 193–233.
6. Paul Grendler, "The University of Padua 1405–1600: A Success Story," *History of Higher Education*, Annual 10 (1990): 7–17, 36–37.
7. On the Jesuit school in Padua, see John Patrick Donnelly, "The Jesuit College at Padua, Growth, Suppression, Attempts at Restoration: 1552–1606," *Archivum Historicum Societatis Iesu* 51 (1982): 45–78; Maurizio Sangalli, *Università accademie gesuiti: Cultura e religione a Padova tra Cinque e Seicento* (Trieste, 2001), vii–xx; and Paul Grendler, *The Universities of the Italian Renaissance* (Baltimore, 2002), 479–483.
8. The account of the events of 1591 is based on the documents published in Antonio Favaro, *Lo Studio di Padova e la Compagnia di Gesù* (Venice, 1878), which represent the university's point of view. These must be supplemented with the research of Donnelly, "The Jesuit College at Padua," 50–57, and Maurizio Sangalli, *Cultura, politica e religione nella Repubblica di Venezia tra Cinque e Seicento: Gesuiti e Somaschi a Venezia*, Istituto Veneto di Scienze, Lettere ed Arti, Memorie: Classe di scienze morali, lettere ed arti 84 (Venice, 1999): 187–276. Also see the introduction by Antonino Poppi in Cesare Cremonini, *Le orazioni* (Padua, 1998), quotation from Cremonini, 64. On the broader political conflicts within the Venetian patriciate over the Jesuits, see William J. Bouwsma, *Venice and the Defense of Republican Liberty: Renaissance Values in the Age of the Counter Reformation* (Berkeley, 1968), 253–254,

and Bouwsma, "Venice and the Political Education of Europe," in *A Usable Past: Essays in European Cultural History* (Berkeley, 1990), 266–291.

9. Maurizio Sangalli, "Cesare Cremonini, la Compagnia di Gesù e la Repubblica di Venezia: Eterodossia e protezione politica," in Ezio Riondato and Antonino Poppi, eds., *Cesare Cremonini: Aspetti del pensiero e scritti: Atti del Convegno di studio (Padova, 26–27 febbraio 1999)*, vol. 1: *Il pensiero* (Padua, 2000), 207–218, quotations on 210. The responses to Cremonini by the five Jesuit fathers are published in Maurizio Sangalli, "Apologie dei Padri Gesuiti contro Cesare Cremonini, 1592," *Atti e Memorie dell'Accademia Patavina di Scienze Lettere ed Arti, anno accademico, 1997–98*, 110, no. 3: Memorie della classe di scienze morali lettere ed arti (Padua, 1997–98): 241–355.

10. Sangalli, "Cesare Cremonini, la Compagnia di Gesù," 213.

11. Bouwsma, *Venice and the Defense of Republican Liberty*, 122–123.

12. John W. O'Malley, *The First Jesuits* (Cambridge, Mass., 1993), 223. The discussion of Jesuit pedagogy is based on O'Malley's account, 200–226.

13. Alison Simmons, "Jesuit Aristotelian Education: The *De Anima* Commentaries," in *The Jesuits: Cultures, Sciences, and the Arts, 1540–1773*, eds. John W. O'Malley, S.J., Gavin Alexander Bailey, Steven J. Harris, and T. Frank Kennedy, S.J. (Toronto, 1999), 522–537.

14. Quoted in Sangalli, "Cesare Cremonini, la Compagnia di Gesù," 213.

15. On salaries and abuses, see Grendler, *The Universities of the Italian Renaissance*, 486–491.

16. Quoted in Donnelly, "The Jesuit College at Padua," 46.

17. Ibid., 77. On anti-Jesuit writing in general, Sabina Pavone, *Le Astuzie dei Gesuiti: Le false Costituzioni della Compagnia di Gesù e la polemica antigesuita nei secoli XVII e XVIII* (Rome, 2000).

18. Bouwsma, *Venice and the Defense of Republican Liberty*, 509–525; Da-

vid Wootton, *Paolo Sarpi: Between Renaissance and Enlightenment* (Cambridge, 1983); Vittorio Frajese, *Sarpi scettico: Stato e chiesa Venezia tra Cinque e Seicento* (Bologna, 1994).

19. Quoted and translated in Bouwsma, *Venice and the Defense of Republican Liberty*, 524–525.

20. On Sarpi's anti-Jesuit writings, see Luigi Lazzerini, "Officina sarpiana: Scritture del Sarpi in materia di Gesuiti," *Rivista di storia della chiesa in Italia* 58 (2004): 29–74.

21. Ezio Riondato, "Cremonini e l'Accademia dei Ricoverati" and Lucia Rossetti, "Cesare Cremonini e la 'nation Germanica aristarum,'" in Riondato and Poppi, *Cesare Cremonini*, 1:9–18 and 131–134, respectively. On the Jesuits and the German students, see Sangalli, *Cultura, politica e religione*, 221–241.

22. The most important counterargument to the Copernican basis for Galileo's trial has been Pietro Redondi's claim that the Inquisition's real concern was Galileo's atomism. See *Galileo Heretic*, trans. Raymond Rosenthal (Princeton, 1987).

23. Leen Spruit, "Cremonini nelle carte del Sant'Uffizio Romano," in Riondato and Poppi, *Cesare Cremonini*, 1:193–205.

24. Antonino Poppi, *Cremonini e Galilei inquisiti a Padova nel 1604: Nuovi documenti d'archivio* (Padua, 1992), document 4, pp. 41–49. On Galileo's career as an astrologer, see H. Darrel Rutkin, "Galileo Astrologer: Astrology and Mathematical Practice in the Late-Sixteenth and Early-Seventeenth Centuries," *Galilaeana* 2 (2005): 107–143.

25. Poppi, *Cremonini e Galilei inquisiti a Padova nel 1604*, 43–44.

26. Ibid., document 5, pp. 55–61, quotation on 59.

27. Ibid., document 9, pp. 70–72; document 10, pp. 73–76; document 12, p. 81; document 15, pp. 88–93.

28. Spruit, "Cremonini nelle carte del Sant'Uffizio Romano," 193–205.

29. Heinrich C. Kuhn, "Cesare Cremonini: Volti e maschere di un

filosofo scomodo per tre secoli e mezzo," in Riondato and Poppi, *Cesare Cremonini*, 1:153–168, quotation on 160, n. 71. Heinrich C. Kuhn, *Venetischer Aristotelismus im Ende der aristotelischen Welt: Aspekte der Welt und des Denkens des Cesare Cremonini (1550–1631)*, Europäische Hochschulschriften 20: Philosophie (Frankfurt, 1996).

30. Kuhn, "Cesare Cremonini," 153.

31. Ibid., 154–155.

32. Aldo Stella, "L'Università di Padova al tempo del Cremonini," in *Cesare Cremonini (1550–1631): Il suo pensiero e il suo tempo, Convegno di Studi Cento 7 aprile 1984* (Cento, 1990), 69–82, and Domenico Bosco, "Cremonini e le origini del libertinismo," ibid., 249–289.

33. John Herman Randall, Jr., *The School of Padua and the Emergence of Modern Science* (Padua, 1961), 62.

34. Randall, *The School of Padua*, 61–65, quotation on 64, n. 40 (translation mine); Fernando Fiorentino, *Cesare Cremonini e il* Tractatus de Paedia (Lecce, 1997), 9, 17, 39–52.

35. Fiorentino, *Cesare Cremonini*, 55.

36. Antonio Lorenzini da Montepulciano, *Discorso . . . intorno all Nuova Stella* (Padua, 1605); Stillman Drake, "Galileo and the Career of Philosophy," *Journal of the History of Ideas* 38 (1977): 19–32.

37. Published in English translation in Stillman Drake, *Galileo against the Philosophers in His* Dialogue *of Cecco di Rochitti (1605) and Considerations of Alimberto Mauri (1606)* (Los Angeles, 1976).

38. Drake, "Galileo and the Career of Philosophy," 27.

39. See Grendler, *The Universities of the Italian Renaissance*, 293–297.

40. Nicholas Davidson, "Unbelief and Atheism in Italy, 1500–1700," in *Atheism from the Reformation to the Enlightenment*, eds. Michael Hunter and David Wootton (Oxford, 1992), 84. Davidson is countering the argument of Lucien Febvre that systematic atheism was not conceivable before the end of the seventeenth century. *The Problem of Unbelief in the Sixteenth Century: The Religion*

of Rabelais (London, 1982), 131–139. See also David Wootton, "Lucien Febvre and the Problem of Unbelief in the Early Modern Period," *Journal of Modern History* 60 (1988): 695–730.

41. Davidson, "Unbelief and Atheism in Italy," 73–74.

42. Kuhn, "Cesare Cremonini," 158–160.

43. Drake, "Galileo and the Career of Philosophy," 22.

44. Galileo Galilei, *Dialogue concerning the Two Chief World Systems—Ptolemaic and Copernican*, trans. Stillman Drake, rev. 2nd ed. (Berkeley, 1967), 111–112.

45. Bosco, "Cremonini e le origini del libertinismo," quotation on 252. On this quotation as the libertine motto, and, more broadly, on the libertine literary phenomenon, see James Grantham Turner, *Schooling Sex: Libertine Literature and Erotic Education in Italy, France, and England 1534–1685* (Oxford, 2003), 84.

46. Quoted in Giorgio Spini, *Ricerca dei libertini: La Teoria dell'impostura delle religioni nel Seicento italiano*, rev. ed. (Florence, 1983), 6.

47. Antonio Daniele, "'Una pura disputa di cose poetiche, senza rancore di sorte alcuna': Alessandro Tassoni, Cesare Cremonini e Giuseppe degli Aromatari," in Riondato and Poppi, *Cesare Cremonini*, 1:19–41, quotation on 26.

2. The Libertines

1. Ferrante Pallavicino, *Il Divortio celeste, cagionato dalle dissolutezze della Sposa Romana & consacrato alla semplicità de' scropolosi Christiani* (Villafranca, 1643), n.p. See also Giorgio Spini, *Ricerca dei libertini: La Teoria dell'impostura delle religioni nel Seicento italiano*, rev. ed. (Florence, 1983), 192. For a bibliography of works by and about Pallavicino, see Laura Coci, "Bibliografia di Ferrante Pallavicino," *Studi secenteschi* 24 (1983): 221–306.

2. Brendan Dooley, *The Social History of Skepticism: Experience and Doubt in Early Modern Culture* (Baltimore, 1999). On the function of Venetian information networks, see Peter Burke, "Early Mod-

ern Venice as a Center of Information and Communication," in *Venice Reconsidered: The History and Civilization of an Italian City-State, 1297–1797,* eds. John Martin and Dennis Romano (Baltimore, 2000), 389–419.

3. Ferrante Pallavicino, *Il Sole ne' pianeti, cioè le grandezze della Serenissima Republica di Venetia* (Padua, 1635).

4. Spini, *Ricerca dei libertini,* 171–172.

5. Donatella Riposio, *Il Laberinto della verità: Aspetti del romanzo libertino del Seicento* (Alessandria, 1995), 5–8.

6. Ellen Rosand, *Opera in Seventeenth-Century Venice* (Berkeley, 1991), 37.

7. Ferrante Pallavicino, *Successi del mondo dell'anno MDCXXXVI* (Venice, 1638), n.p., discusses the need to keep the truth hidden.

8. Girolamo Brusoni [aka Iacopo Gaddi], *Le Glorie degl' Incogniti o vero gli huomini illustri dell'Accademia de' signori Incogniti di Venetia* (Venice, 1647).

9. Paolo Marangon, "Aristotelismo e Cartesianesimo: Filosofia accademica e libertini," in *Storia della cultura Veneta,* eds. Girolamo Arnaldi and Manlio Pastore Stocchi, vol. 4, part 2: *Il Seicento* (Vicenza, 1984), 96–97.

10. Spini, *Ricerca dei libertini,* 155; Maria Assunta Del Torre, "La trattazione 'De Anima,'" in *Studi su Cesare Cremonini: Cosmologia e logica nel tardo aristotelismo padovano* (Padua, 1968), 35–49; Wendy Heller, "Tacitus Incognito: Opera as History in *L'Incoronazione di Poppea,*" *Journal of American Musicological Society* 52 (1999): 45–46.

11. Spini, *Ricerca dei libertini,* 164.

12. Wendy Heller notes how the *Novelties* were, in part, a response to Arcangela Tarabotti's criticisms of the misogyny of the Incogniti. "'O delle donne miserabil sesso': Tarabotti, Ottavia, and *L'Incoronazione di Poppea,*" *Il saggiatore musicale* 7 (2000): 21. For a bibliography on Tarabotti, see p. 5, n. 1. See also Heller, "'O castità bugiarda': Cavalli's 'Didone' and the Convention of Abandonment," in *A Woman Scorn'd: Responses to the Dido Myth,* ed. Mi-

chael Burden (London, 1998), 169–225. On the broader context of Venetian writing about women, see Lynn Lara Westwater, "The Disquieting Voice: Women's Writing and Antifeminism in Seventeenth-Century Venice" (Ph.D. diss., University of Chicago, 2003).

13. Bernard Aikema, *Pietro della Vecchia and the Heritage of the Renaissance in Venice* (Florence, 1990), 58 and fig. 109.

14. Benzoni, "La Vita intellettuale," in *Storia di Venezia dalle origini alla caduta della Serenissima*, vol. 7: *La Venezia barocca*, eds. Gino Benzoni and Gaetano Cozzi (Rome, 1997), 850.

15. Ibid., 851.

16. Rosalie Colie, *Paradoxia Epidemica: The Renaissance Tradition of Paradox* (Princeton, 1966).

17. Mauro Calcagno, "Signifying Nothing: On the Aesthetics of Pure Voice in Early Venetian Opera," *Journal of Musicology* 20 (2003): 466–475.

18. The judgment about the proto-Enlightenment character of the libertines is that of Armando Marchi, the editor of Ferrante Pallavicino, *Il Corriero svaligiato* (Parma, 1984), vi.

19. Le Père F. Garasse, *Doctrine curieuse des beaux espr.* (Paris, 1623), 1–2; Spini, *Ricerca dei libertini*, 149–150.

20. Marangon, "Aristotelismo e Cartesianesimo," 106–111; James Grantham Turner, *Schooling Sex: Libertine Literature and Erotic Education in Italy, France, and England, 1534–1685* (Oxford, 2003), 88–105; Spini, *Ricerca dei libertini*, p. 161, n. 10.

21. On Rocco, see Benzoni, "La Vita intellettuale," 851–852; on the Pietro della Vecchia painting, see Aikema, *Pietro della Vecchia*, 61–62; on the connection between the *novella* and the opera, see Lorenzo Bianconi and Thomas Walker, "Production, Consumption and Political Function of Seventeenth-Century Opera," *Early Music History* 4 (1984): 267; for the translated quotation, see Rosand, *Opera in Seventeenth-Century Venice*, 59.

22. Archivio di Stato, Venezia, S. Uffizio, Processi, busta 103, quoted in Spini, *Ricerca dei libertini*, 163–164.

23. Spini, *Ricerca dei libertini*, 158–161.

24. The Italian verb translated as "to cheat" is *ingannare*, which was one of the favorite words of the Incogniti. Gio. Francesco Loredano, *Bizzarrie academiche* (Venice, 1654), 136–139.

25. Robert Finlay, "The Venetian Republic as a Gerontocracy: Age and Politics in the Renaissance," *Journal of Medieval and Renaissance Studies* 8 (1978): 157–178.

26. Girolamo Brusoni, *Vita di Ferrante Pallavicino* (Venice, 1655), 8.

27. Armando Marchi, introduction to Pallavicino, *Il Corriero svaligiato*, viii–xxiv.

28. Laura Coci, "Ferrante a Venezia: Nuovi documenti d'archivio," *Studi secenteschi* 27 (1986): 317–324.

29. Laura Coci, "Ferrante a Venezia: Nuovi documenti d'archivio (II)," *Studi secenteschi* 28 (1987): 302–303.

30. Ferrante Pallavicino, *Baccinata overo Battarella per le Api Barberine in occasione della mossa delle armi di N.S. Papa Urbano Ottavo contro Parma* (n.p., 1642); Pallavicino, *Dialogo molto curioso e degno tra due gentilhuomini Acanzi, cioè soldati volontari dell'Altezze Serenissime di Modona e Parma, sopra la Guerra che detti prencipi fanno contra il Papa, in cui con ogni verità toccansi le cose di detta Guerra, su la fine leggesi anco un breve discorso fatto da Pasquino a Papa Urbano VIII* (n.p. [1642]); *La Retorica delle puttane, composta conforme li precetti di Cipriano, dedicate alla Università delle Cortegiane più celebri* (Cambrai, 1642). I consulted the modern edition of *La Retorica*, ed. Laura Coci (Parma, 1992).

31. See Riposio, *Il Laberinto della verità*, 18.

32. Pallavicino, *La Retorica delle puttane*; Benzoni, "La Vita intellettuale," 850, 852–853; and Turner, *Schooling Sex*, 74–87.

33. Turner, *Schooling Sex*, 75. On Jesuit rhetoric, see Jean Dietz Moss and William A. Wallace, *Rhetoric and Dialectic in the Time of Galileo* (Washington, D.C., 2003), 111–186, and Marc Fumaroli, "The

Fertility and the Shortcomings of Renaissance Rhetoric: The Jesuit Case," in *The Jesuits: Cultures, Sciences, and the Arts, 1540–1773,* eds. John W. O'Malley, S.J., Gavin Alexander Bailey, Steven J. Harris, and T. Frank Kennedy, S.J. (Toronto, 1999), 90–106.

34. C. Poggiali, *Memorie per la storia della letteratura di Piacenza* (Piacenza, 1789), 2:186, as cited in Raffaello Urbinati, *Ferrante Pallavicino: Il Flagello dei Barberini* (Rome, 2004), 139 (the account that follows in text is based on pp. 135–169 of Urbinati); Brusoni, *Vita di Ferrante Pallavicino,* 19–23; and Giovanni Francesco Loredan (?), *L'Anima di Ferrante Pallavicino, vigilia prima* (Lyons, n.d.), 21.

35. Benzoni, "La Vita intellettuale," 856–857.

36. Pallavicino, *Il Corriero svaligiato,* 10–15. I have taken the English translation from appendix 2 of Arcangela Tarabotti, *Paternal Tyranny,* ed. and trans. Letizia Panizza (Chicago, 2004), 159.

37. Tarabotti, *Paternal Tyranny,* 121–22.

38. Ibid., 147. Tarabotti has her dates wrong, given that *Il Corriero svaligiato* appeared after Pallavicino's arrest but before his execution.

39. Ibid., 148.

40. Panizza, introduction, ibid., 8–9, and "Introductory Essay" in Arcangela Tarabotti, *Che le donne siano della spezie degli uomini / Women Are No Less Rational Than Men* (London, 1994), xii–xv, quotation on xv.

41. Panizza, introduction to Tarabotti, *Paternal Tyranny,* 1.

42. Ibid., 66.

43. Ibid., 37–38.

44. I have closely followed Panizza's introduction here. Quotations are from ibid., 14–15.

3. The Librettists

1. Giovanni Francesco Busenello, *Delle hore ociose* (Venice, 1656), 3r. The quotation is taken from the translation by Wendy Heller,

Emblems of Eloquence: Opera and Women's Voices in Seventeenth-Century Venice (Berkeley, 2003), 136. Parts of this chapter derive from Edward Muir, "Why Venice? Venetian Society and the Success of Early Opera," *Journal of Interdisciplinary History* 36 (2006): 331–354. See the comments on that article in the same issue by Dennis Romano, "Commentary: Why Opera? The Politics of an Emerging Genre," and Ellen Rosand, "Commentary: Seventeenth-Century Venetian Opera as *Fondamente nuove*," 401–409 and 411–417, respectively.

2. Alessandra Chiarelli, "*L'Incoronazione di Poppea o Il Nerone:* Problemi di filologia testuale," *Rivista italiana di musicologia* 9 (1974): 117–151; Alan Curtis, "*La Poppea Impasticciata,* or Who Wrote the Music to *L'Incoronazione* (1643)?" *Journal of the American Musicological Society* 42 (1989): 23–54; Iain Fenlon and Peter N. Miller, *The Song of the Soul: Understanding* Poppea (London, 1992), 3.

3. Anne Ridler, *The Operas of Monteverdi* (London, 1992), 192. Translation mine.

4. The Venetian word for prostitute, *meretrice*, was applied to any woman in a sexual relationship with one or more men outside marriage, whether or not the exchange of money for sex was involved. By that definition, Poppea was a *meretrice*.

5. Ellen Rosand, "Seneca and the Interpretation of *L'Incoronazione di Poppea*," *Journal of the American Musicological Society* 38 (1985): 34–71; Tim Carter, "Re-Reading *Poppea*: Some Thoughts on Music and Meaning in Monteverdi's Last Opera," *Journal of the Royal Musical Association* 122 (1997): 173–204; Robert C. Ketterer, "Neoplatonic Light and Dramatic Genre in Busenello's *L'Incoronazione di Poppea* and Noris's *Il Ripudio d'Ottavia*," *Music and Letters* 80 (1999): 1–22.

6. Iain Fenlon and Peter Miller, "Public Vice, Private Virtue," in *Claudio Monteverdi: Studi e prospettive*, eds. Paola Besutti, Teresa M. Gialdroni, and Rodolfo Baroncini (Florence, 1998), 134.

7. Fenlon and Miller, *The Song of the Soul*, 92. See also the reviews of

Fenlon and Miller, *The Song of the Soul*, by Robert Holzer in *Cambridge Opera Journal* 5 (1993): 79–92.

8. Francesco Degrada, "Il Teatro di Claudio Monteverdi: Gli studi sullo stile," in *Claudio Monteverdi: Studi e prospettive*, eds. Paola Besutti, Teresa M. Gialdroni, and Rodolfo Baroncini (Florence, 1998), 274–277.

9. Review by Susan K. McClary in *Music and Letters* 72 (1992): 280.

10. Heller, *Emblems of Eloquence*, 177. See also Heller, "'O delle donne miserabil sesso': Tarabotti, Ottavia, and *L'Incoronazione di Poppea*," *Il Saggiatore musicale* 7 (2000): 5–46; Heller, "Tacitus Incognito: Opera as History in *L'Incoronazione di Poppea*," *Journal of American Musicological Society* 52 (1999): 39–96; Heller "Poppea's Legacy: The Julio-Claudians on the Venetian Stage," *Journal of Interdisciplinary History* 36 (2006): 379–399. The debate on the interpretation of *Poppea* is summarized in Degrada, "Il Teatro di Claudio Monteverdi," 274–282.

11. Virgina Cox, "The Single Self: Feminist Thought and the Marriage Market in Early Modern Venice," *Renaissance Quarterly* 48 (1995): 513–576.

12. Laura Jane McGough, *Extreme Beauty: Sexuality and Disease in Early Modern Venice* (Baltimore, forthcoming). See also Monica Chojnacka, *Working Women of Early Modern Venice* (Baltimore, 2001).

13. Stanley Chojnacki, *Women and Men in Renaissance Venice: Twelve Essays on Patrician Society* (Baltimore, 2000), 56, 63–65, quotation on 63.

14. Patricia Labalme, "Sodomy and Venetian Justice in the Renaissance," *Legal History Review* 52 (1984): 217–254; Guido Ruggiero, *The Boundaries of Eros: Sex Crime and Sexuality in Renaissance Venice* (New York, 1985), 109–145, and Ruggiero, *Binding Passions: Tales of Magic, Marriage, and Power at the End of the Renaissance* (New York, 1993), 175–176, 256–258; Michael Rocke, "Gender and Sexual Culture in Renaissance Italy," in *Gender and Society in Renaissance Italy*,

eds. Judith C. Brown and Robert C. Davis (London, 1998), 150–170; Julius Kirshner, "Family and Marriage: A Socio-Legal Perspective," in *Italy in the Age of the Renaissance 1300–1550*, ed. John M. Najemy (Oxford, 2004), 82–102.

15. James C. Davis, *A Venetian Family and Its Fortune, 1500–1900* (Philadelphia, 1975), 93–106; Chojnacki, *Women and Men in Renaissance Venice*, 244–256. For a self-conscious discussion of restricted marriage by aristocrats in Friuli, see Edward Muir, "The Double Binds of Manly Revenge," in *Gender Rhetorics: Postures of Dominance and Submission in Human History*, ed. Richard C. Trexler (Binghamton, N.Y., 1994), 65–82.

16. Jutta Gisela Sperling, who collected these data, admits, "This figure is too high to be realistic, but it indicates a clear trend." See Sperling, *Convents and the Body Politic in Late Renaissance Venice* (Chicago, 1999), 28, table 2. See also Federica Ambrosini, "Toward a Social History of Women in Venice: From the Renaissance to the Enlightenment," in *Venice Reconsidered: The History and Civilization of an Italian City-State, 1297–1797*, eds. John Martin and Dennis Romano (Baltimore, 2000), 423–424.

17. Sperling, *Convents*, 18–26.

18. James C. Davis, *The Decline of the Venetian Nobility as a Ruling Class* (Baltimore, 1962); Volker Hunecki, *Der venezianische Adel am Ende der Republik (1646–1797): Demographie, Familie, Haushalt* (Tübingen, 1995), 357–358, 383, Italian trans. Benedetta Heinemann Campana, *Il Patriziato veneziano alla fine della Repubblica, 1646–1797: Demografia, familia, ménage* (Rome, 1997).

19. Claude V. Palisca, *The Florentine Camerata: Documentary Studies and Translations* (New Haven, 1989). Palisca argues that rather than being an academy, the Camerata was an informal body in which competing ideas about musical theory circulated—see 1–12.

20. Vincenzo Galilei, *Dialogue on Ancient and Modern Music*, trans. and annot. Claude V. Palisca (New Haven, 2003), quotation on xvii.

21. Ibid., lix.

22. Ellen Rosand, *Opera in Seventeenth-Century Venice* (Berkeley, 1991), 1.

23. Statistics based on a private communication from Ellen Rosand.

24. James H. Johnson, *Listening in Paris: A Cultural History* (Berkeley, 1995), 10.

25. Quoted in Beth L. Glixon and Jonathan E. Glixon, *Inventing the Business of Opera: The Impresario and His World in Seventeenth-Century Venice* (Oxford, 2006), 302.

26. Rosand, *Opera in Seventeenth-Century Venice*, 1.

27. This opinion is confirmed in the most important study of early commercial opera, Glixon and Glixon, *Inventing the Business of Opera*.

28. Ibid., 19.

29. Carmelo Alberti, "L'Invenzione del teatro," in *Storia di Venezia dalle origini alla caduta della Serenissima*, 7: *La Venezia barocca*, eds. Gino Benzoni and Gaetano Cozzi (Rome, 1997), 726.

30. Archivio di Stato, Venice, Consiglio dei Dieci, Misti, reg. 32, c. 55v, published in Alberti, "L'Invenzione del teatro," 706–707.

31. Lionello Venturi, "Le Compagnie della Calza (sec. 15–17)," *Nuovo Archivio Veneto*, n.s. 16, no. 2 (1908): 161–221, and 17, no. 1 (1909): 140–233. Matteo Casini is preparing a more up-to-date study of the companies.

32. Quoted in Alberti, "L'Invenzione," p. 746, n. 2.

33. Linda L. Carroll, *Angelo Beolco (Il Ruzante)* (Boston, 1990); Carroll, "Carnival Themes in the Plays of Ruzante," *Italian Culture* 5 (1984): 55–66.

34. Marino Sanuto, *I diarii*, eds. Federico Stefani, Guglielmo Berchet, and Nicolò Barozzi (Venice, 1893), vol. 37, cols. 559–560.

35. Eugene J. Johnson, "The Short, Lascivious Lives of Two Venetian Theaters, 1580–85," *Renaissance Quarterly* 55 (2002): 946.

36. Quoted ibid., 938, n. 11.

37. Jonathan E. Glixon and Beth L. Glixon, "Oil and Opera Don't Mix: The Biography of S. Aponal, a Seventeenth-Century Vene-

tian Opera Theater," in *Music in the Theater, Church, and Villa: Essays in Honor of Robert Lamar Weaver and Norma Wright Weaver,* ed. Susan Parisi (Warren, Michigan, 2000), 137; Glixon and Glixon, *Inventing the Business of Opera,* 298–302.

38. Quoted and translated in Johnson, "The Short Lascivious Lives," 942.

39. Quoted and translated ibid., 948, 949.

40. Ibid., 938–939, 955–956.

41. Gaetano Cozzi, "Dalla riscoperta della pace all'inestinguibile sogno di dominio," in *Storia di Venezia dalle origini alla caduta della Serenissima,* vol. 7: *La Venezia barocca,* eds. Gino Benzoni and Gaetano Cozzi (Rome, 1997), 49.

42. I mean "playful" in Johan Huizinga's sense of "serious play" as the source of cultural innovation. Johan Huizinga, *Homo Ludens: A Study of the Play Element in Culture* (New York, 1970).

43. Gino Benzoni, "Le Accademie," in *Storia della cultura Veneta,* eds. Girolamo Arnaldi and Manlo Pastore Stocchi, vol. 4, part 1: *Il Seicento* (Vicenza, 1983), 135. On the sixteenth-century academies, see David S. Chambers, "The Earlier 'Academies' in Italy"; Lina Bolzoni, "'Rendere visibile il sapere': L'Accademia veneziana fra modernità e utopia"; and Iain Fenlon, "Zarlino and the Accademia Venetiana," all in *Italian Academies of the Sixteenth Century,* eds. D. S. Chambers and F. Quiviger (London, 1995), 1–14, 61–78, 79–90 respectively.

44. Rosand, *Opera in Seventeenth-Century Venice,* 88–109.

45. On opera between its theoretical invention in Florence and the first commercial production in Venice in 1637, see Paolo Fabbri, "Diffusione dell'Opera," in *Musica in Scena: Storia dello spettacolo musicale,* ed. Alberto Basso, vol. 1: *Il Teatro musicale dalle origini al primo Settecento* (Turin, 1995), 106–107.

46. Quoted and translated in Rosand, *Opera in Seventeenth-Century Venice,* 42.

47. Quoted and translated ibid., 155.

48. Robert C. Davis, *The War of the Fists: Popular Culture and Public Violence in Late Renaissance Venice* (New York, 1994).

49. Giovanni Morelli and Thomas R. Walker, "Tre controversie intorno al San Cassiano," in *Venezia e il melodrama nel Seicento,* ed. Maria Teresa Muraro (Florence, 1976), 103.

50. Alberti, "L'Invenzione," 719–22. On Venetian pageantry, see Edward Muir, *Civic Ritual in Renaissance Venice* (Princeton, 1981).

51. Alberti, "L'Invenzione," 719.

52. Glixon and Glixon, "Oil and Opera," 138.

53. G. M. Pachtler, S.J., *Ratio studiorum et institutiones scholasticae Societatis Jesu per Germaniam olim vigentes* (Berlin, 1887–1894), 3:472, as translated in William H. McCabe, S.J., *An Introduction to the Jesuit Theater,* ed. Louis J. Oldani, S.J. (St. Louis, 1983), 11–12.

54. Marc Fumaroli, "The Fertility and the Shortcomings of Renaissance Rhetoric: The Jesuit Case," in *The Jesuits: Cultures, Sciences, and the Arts, 1540–1773,* ed. John W. O'Malley, S.J., Gavin Alexander Bailey, Steven J. Harris, and T. Frank Kennedy, S.J. (Toronto, 1999), 96. See also Ernest Boysse, *Le théâtre des jésuites* (Paris, 1880).

55. Liam M. Brockey, "Jesuit Pastoral Theater on an Urban Stage: Lisbon, 1588–1593," *Journal of Early Modern History* 9 (2005): 3–50.

56. Pachtler, *Ratio studiorum,* 2:272, as translated in McCabe, *Introduction to the Jesuit Theater,* 14.

57. Elissa B. Weaver, *Convent Theatre in Early Modern Italy: Spiritual Fun and Learning for Women* (Cambridge, 2002).

58. Richard Andrews, "Isabella Andreini and Others: Women on Stage in the Late Cinquecento," in *Women in Italian Renaissance Culture and Society,* ed. Letizia Panizza (Oxford, 2000), 316–333.

59. Salvianus, *On the Government of God,* trans. Eva M. Sanford (New York, 1930), 163. See also Jonas Barish, *The Antitheatrical Prejudice* (Berkeley, 1981), 80.

60. Barish, *The Antitheatrical Prejudice,* 115.

61. Joseph Connors, "Chi era Ottonelli?" in *Pietro da Cortona,* eds.

Christoph Luitpold Frommel and Sebastian Schütze (Milan, 1998), 21–27. Gian Domenico Ottonelli's work is *Della Christiana moderatione del teatro* (Florence, 1655).

62. Gian Vincenzo Gravina, "Della tragedia" (Naples, 1715) in *Scritti critici e teorici*, ed. Amedeo Quondam (Bari, 1973), 507, quoted and trans. in Mauro Calcagno, "Signifying Nothing: On the Aesthetics of Pure Voice in Early Venetian Opera," *Journal of Musicology* 20 (2003): 461.

63. Calcagno, "Signifying Nothing," 463.

64. Giovan Francesco Loredan, *Discorsi academici de' Signori Incogniti* (Venice, 1635), 267–287.

65. See also the argument that disorientation in the arts marked the end of the Renaissance, in William J. Bouwsma, *The Waning of the Renaissance, 1550–1640* (New Haven, 2000), esp. 129–142.

66. Calcagno, "Signifying Nothing," 472–473.

67. Glixon and Glixon make a similar point about the opera box in *Inventing the Business of Opera*, 19.

68. Domenico Sella, "Crisis and Transformation in Venetian Trade," in *Crisis and Change in the Venetian Economy in the Sixteenth and Seventeenth Centuries*, ed. Brian S. Pullan (London, 1968), 88–105.

69. Mauro Calcagno, "Censoring *Eliogabalo* in Seventeenth-Century Venice," *Journal of Interdisciplinary History* 36 (2006): 355–377.

70. See, however, on the survival of skeptical, libertine, and heterodox ideas in Venice in the late seventeenth and eighteenth centuries, Federico Barbierato, "La Bottega del cappellaio: Libri proibiti, libertinismo e suggestioni massoniche nel '700 Veneto," *Studi veneziani* 44 (2002): 327–361; Barbierato, "Dissenso religioso, discussione politica e mercato dell'informazione a Venezia fra Seicento e Settecento," *Società e storia* 102 (2003): 709–757; and Barbierato, "Luterani, Calvinisti e libertini: Dissidenza religiosa a Venezia nel secondo Seicento," *Studi storici* 46 (2005): 797–844.

Index

Index

Index

Index

Index

Music, theories of, 121–122, 126, 132–133, 138, 144–145

Naples, 143
Naudé, Gabriel, 56–57
Nero, 107, 111–115, 146
Netherlands, 16, 98
Nothingness, discourses on, 76–79

O'Malley, John, 30
Opera, 2–3, 5, 7, 9–10, 22–23, 30, 71, 107, 111–148
Opera houses, 117, 122–123, 125–126, 128–135, 138, 145–146, 148
Ottoman Empire, 121, 133, 136–137, 147
Ottonelli, Gian Domenico, 142–143

Padua: university in, 2, 5–6, 15, 18, 21, 23–29, 31–33, 35–39, 64, 68, 72; Jesuit college in, 21, 24–27, 29–31, 33–35, 38, 139–140, 147
Paedia, 48–50, 52
Palermo, 143
Palladio, Andrea, 80
Palladio, Enrico, 81
Pallavicino, Ferrante, 22, 63–65, 67–70, 86, 89–91, 93–95, 97–101, 103, 106–107, 111, 121; *The Celestial Divorce*, 63–65, 90, 94, 98, 107; *The Post-Boy Robbed of His Bag*, 86, 89–90, 99–100; *Rhetoric of Whores*, 90, 93–95, 143; *The Sun in the Planets*, 68
Panizza, Letizia, 103, 105–106
Papacy, 2–3, 5, 26, 28, 33, 36, 44, 63–64, 67, 86, 89, 94, 97–100, 111, 130–131, 143
Parental tyranny, 3, 22, 103–105, 119

Paris, 5, 27, 29–30, 54, 97, 123
Parma, 63, 67, 89
Patrizi, Francesco, 7
Paul, 64, 78
Pedagogy, theories of, 21–22, 24–25, 28–30, 33, 35, 49
Pederasty, 3, 80–83, 93
Persio, Antonio, 130
Petrarca, Francesco, 57
Philosophy, 8, 28–31, 35, 40, 43, 47, 49–51, 53, 56–57, 90, 93, 145
Piagnoni, Silvestro, 38–39
Piccolomini, Francesco, 26, 48
Pighetti, Giacomo, 101
Pisa, 81
Plato, 85
Poetry, theories of, 57–58, 79
Polanco, Juan Alfonso de, 29
Poland, 5, 28, 48
Pomponazzi, Pietro, 28, 30, 39–40, 48
Poppea (Poppaea), 107, 112–114, 117
Possevino, Antonio, 36
Prague, 36
Private teaching, 32
Procuratie Vecchie, 128
Protestantism, 4–5, 16, 28–29, 36, 53, 64, 67, 69–70, 98, 141–143
Ptolemy (Claudius Ptolemaeus), 43
Puritans, 9, 141–143
Pythagoras, 75

Randall, John Herman, Jr., 48
Renza, Anna, 132
Republicanism, 3, 28, 85–86, 105
Rhetoric, theories of, 57, 85, 90, 93–94, 99, 143–145

Index

Index